CW00502350

Greek

THE AUSTRALIAN Women's Weekly

Greek

acp books

Contents

Introduction 6
Greek essentials 8
Mezze 10
Soups 126
Salads 142
Mains 182
  Chicken + Rabbit 184
  Seafood 218
  Lamb + Goat 254
  Vegetarian 302
Celebration 322
Sweets 342
Glossary 386
Index 392
Conversion chart 399

For the Greeks, food is a ritual. An experience that must be shared with family and friends. It is about love, spirituality and philosophy and as one of the most ancient cuisines, its culinary traditions have been celebrated for thousands of years. Their food is a reflection of their warmth and generosity.

With 20 percent of Greece made up of islands and no part of the mainland more than a few hundred kilometres from the sea, fish and seafood are a popular part of the Greek diet. The rocky terrain has meant that goats and sheep have thrived there and this is evident in traditional dishes such as lamb fillo pie, goat and capsicum stew and roasted lamb shoulder. There are also the gorgeous sheep's and goat's milk cheeses most famously of course fetta, a key ingredient in the iconic greek salad. The climate is perfect for growing olive and lemon trees, producing two of the most important elements of Greek cooking.

Greeks generally dine late at night when the temperature has cooled down. They sit and eat mezze, drink spirits and wine and talk for hours. The mezze is a romantic notion employed by the Greeks to not only complement and enhance the taste of the drink but to provide the backdrop for a social gathering. Mezze are little plates shared by everyone at the table and unlike appetisers are not intended to whet the appetite for the next meal, but to be experienced as a meal in themselves. The variety of a mezze spread is diverse and adaptable. With everything from cheese fillo triangles to prawn souvlakia and meatballs in tomato sauce, Greek mezze caters to everyone's personal preferences.

It is not surprising that a culture so focused on food, family and celebration holds great enthusiasm for big festivals and religious holidays. The most notable in the Greek calendar is Easter. It is a colourful and vibrant time where streets and homes are decorated with painted eggs, and food is at the centre of all festivities.

This book is full of delicious Greek fare to share with your loved ones. Adopt the Greek eating culture to evoke laughter, happiness and love in your kitchen. Be inspired by Greek hospitality and cherish the process at every stage of cooking, for this food is about more than just sustenance: it is a celebration of life.

Greek essentials

FETTA CHEESE

Traditionally made with sheep's milk, now most often cow's milk. It is shaped into large blocks which are salted, sliced and salted again, then packed in whey for a month or so. It ends up firm, sharp-flavoured and salty. Packed in brine, it should be eaten within a day or two of purchase.

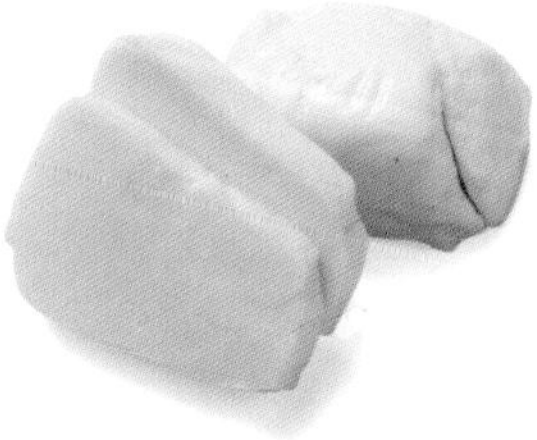

HALOUMI CHEESE

This Cypriot cheese is often used in Greek cooking. It's a firm, traditionally sheep-milk cheese (also goat's or cow's-milk varieties) with a minty, salty flavour; it does not break down when cooked, however it should be eaten while still warm as it becomes tough and rubbery on cooling.

KALAMATA OLIVES

Large black olives with a firm flesh and a meaty flavour; named after the city of Kalamata in Greece. They are available preserved in vinegar or olive oil, and whole or pitted.

RIGANI

Dried Greek oregano, often sold in bunches. Store dried herbs away from heat or light in airtight packets or containers; do not store in the fridge as transferring between a cold fridge and a warm kitchen can cause condensation inside the packet and spoil its contents.

VINE LEAVES

Fresh or preserved grapevine leaves, used for wrapping fillings (dolmades) or lining dishes with savoury mixtures. Preserved leaves are packed in brine so should be rinsed and dried before use. Fresh leaves should be softened in boiling water for a minute until pliable, then dried.

TAHINI

A sesame seed paste; used in dips such as baba ghanoush (eggplant dip) and hummus (chickpea dip). It is available from health food stores, the health food section in most supermarkets and Middle Eastern food stores.

GREEK-STYLE YOGURT

This yogurt has been strained in a cloth (traditionally muslin), to remove the whey and to give it a creamy consistency. It's ideal for use in dips and dressings.

FILLO PASTRY

Paper-thin sheets of raw pastry; are used by brushing with oil or melted butter and stacking one on another, then cutting and folding as the recipe directs. This creates a layered, crackling-crisp, airy crust or wrapping for small pastries such as spanakopita.

Mezze

Artichoke and asparagus fritters with olive relish

170g (5½ ounces) asparagus, trimmed, chopped finely
280g (9 ounces) canned artichokes in brine, drained, chopped finely
2 eggs
½ cup (40g) finely grated kefalotyri cheese
¼ cup (35g) self-raising flour
2 tablespoons finely chopped fresh mint
vegetable oil, for shallow frying

olive relish
½ cup (60g) seeded green olives, chopped finely
½ cup (60g) seeded black olives, chopped finely
¼ cup finely chopped fresh flat-leaf parsley
1 tablespoon finely chopped fresh chives
1 tablespoon olive oil
1 tablespoon lemon juice

1 Make olive relish.
2 Combine asparagus, artichoke, eggs, cheese, flour and mint in medium bowl.
3 Heat oil in large frying pan; shallow-fry heaped tablespoons of fritter mixture, in batches, until browned all over and cooked through. Drain on absorbent paper.
4 Serve fritters hot with olive relish.
olive relish Combine ingredients in small bowl.

prep + cook time 40 minutes **makes** 15
nutritional count per fritter 4.6g total fat (1.2g saturated fat); 288kJ (69 cal); 3.8g carbohydrate; 2.9g protein; 0.8g fibre
tip When shallow-frying, the oil should come halfway up the sides of the fritters. Turn halfway through cooking to brown all over.

Zucchini fritters with skordalia

4 medium zucchini (480g)
2 teaspoons salt
peanut oil, for deep-frying
skordalia
4 slices stale white sandwich bread (180g), crusts removed
4 cloves garlic, crushed
½ cup (125ml) olive oil
1 tablespoon lemon juice
1 tablespoon water, approximately
batter
1 cup (150g) self-raising flour
¾ cup (180ml) warm water
1 tablespoon olive oil
1 egg yolk

1 Cut zucchini into 1cm (½-inch) diagonal slices. Place zucchini in colander, sprinkle with salt; stand 30 minutes. Rinse under cold water; drain on absorbent paper.
2 Meanwhile, make skordalia.
3 Make batter.
4 Heat oil in large saucepan. Dip zucchini into batter; carefully lower into hot oil. Deep-fry zucchini until browned and crisp; drain on absorbent paper.
5 Serve zucchini fritters immediately with skordalia.
skordalia Briefly dip bread into a bowl of cold water, then gently squeeze out liquid. Blend or process bread and garlic until combined. With motor operating, gradually add oil, juice and enough of the water, in a thin steady stream, until mixture is smooth and thick. Transfer to serving bowl.
batter Sift flour into medium bowl; whisk in combined remaining ingredients until smooth. Stand batter 10 minutes.

prep + cook time 1 hour (+ standing) **serves** 6
nutritional count per serving 28g total fat (4.2g saturated fat); 1601kJ (383 cal); 26.5g carbohydrate; 5.4g protein; 3g fibre
tip If batter thickens too much after standing, whisk in a little extra water to give it a coating consistency.

Fetta and spinach stuffed potato balls

450g (14½ ounces) sebago potatoes, chopped coarsely
180g (5½ ounces) spinach, trimmed, shredded finely
150g (4½ ounces) fetta cheese, crumbled
50g (1½ ounces) butter
⅔ cup (160ml) water
1 teaspoon salt
1 cup (150g) plain (all-purpose) flour
2 eggs
vegetable oil, for deep-frying

1 Boil, steam or microwave potato until tender; drain. Mash potato in large bowl; cover to keep warm.
2 Meanwhile, boil, steam or microwave spinach until just wilted; drain. When cool enough to handle, squeeze excess liquid from spinach. Combine in medium bowl with cheese.
3 Melt butter in medium saucepan, add the water and salt; bring to the boil. Remove from heat; immediately stir in flour. Using a wooden spoon, beat until mixture forms a smooth ball. Beat in eggs and potato until smooth.
4 Using floured hands, roll level tablespoons of dough into balls; use finger to press hole into centre of each ball. Fill holes with level teaspoons of spinach mixture; roll potato balls gently to enclose filling.
5 Heat oil in large saucepan; deep-fry balls, in batches, until browned lightly. Drain on absorbent paper.

prep + cook time 1 hour 10 minutes **makes** 30
nutritional count per ball 5.1g total fat (2g saturated fat); 293kJ (70 cal); 3.8g carbohydrate; 2.1g protein; 0.5g fibre
tip You can also use lasoda or pink-eye potatoes for this recipe.

Fried chilli prawns with garlic and lemon yogurt

vegetable oil, for deep-frying
500g (1 pound) uncooked small prawns (shrimp)
1 cup (150g) plain (all-purpose) flour
1 teaspoon ground chilli
garlic and lemon yogurt
¾ cup (210g) greek-style yogurt
1 clove garlic, crushed
1 teaspoon finely grated lemon rind
1 tablespoon lemon juice

1 Make garlic and lemon yogurt.
2 Heat vegetable oil in medium saucepan or wok. Toss unshelled prawns in combined flour and chilli; shake away excess. Deep-fry prawns, in batches, until browned lightly. Drain on absorbent paper. Season with salt and a little extra ground chilli to taste.
3 Serve prawns with yogurt and lemon wedges.
garlic and lemon yogurt Combine ingredients in small bowl; season to taste.

prep + cook time 20 minutes **serves** 6 as a starter
nutritional count per serving 8.2g total fat (2.7g saturated fat); 866kJ (207 cal); 12.9g carbohydrate; 20g protein; 0.7g fibre

Fish croquettes

1 medium brown onion (150g), quartered
8 cloves
2 cloves garlic, halved
2 bay leaves
2 cups (500ml) milk
500g (1 pound) skinless white fish fillets, chopped coarsely
3 medium potatoes (600g), chopped coarsely
½ cup (60g) seeded green olives, chopped coarsely
¾ cup (110g) plain (all-purpose) flour
15 canned, drained anchovy fillets, halved lengthways
vegetable oil, for deep-frying

1 Stud onion quarters with cloves. Place onion, garlic, bay leaves and milk in medium saucepan; bring to simmer, add fish, cook over low heat about 5 minutes. Remove fish from milk mixture to large bowl. Flake fish, discard bones.
2 Meanwhile, bring milk mixture to the boil, add potato; cook, covered, about 15 minutes or until tender. Remove potato from milk mixture, add to fish; mash coarsely. Strain milk mixture into jug; discard bay leaf and cloves from onion. Finely chop onion and garlic, add to fish mixture with olives. Stir sifted flour and ¾ cup (180ml) of the reserved milk into fish mixture, in several batches. Season.
3 Roll 2 heaped tablespoonfuls of fish mixture into balls; place on baking-paper-lined tray. Refrigerate 1 hour. Make an indent in balls, push a rolled-up anchovy half inside each ball; roll balls into ovals to enclose anchovies.
4 Heat oil in large saucepan or wok. Deep-fry croquettes, in batches, until browned; drain on absorbent paper.
5 Serve croquettes with lemon wedges.

prep + cook time 1 hour 20 minutes (+ refrigeration) **makes** 30
nutritional count per croquette 5.2g total fat (1g saturated fat); 385kJ (92 cal); 5.8g carbohydrate; 5.3g protein; 0.6g fibre
tip We used ling in this recipe, but any firm white fish fillets will be fine.

Skordalia

3 medium potatoes (600g), unpeeled
3 cloves garlic
½ teaspoon salt
½ cup (125ml) olive oil
¼ cup (60ml) lemon juice
½ cup (125ml) milk

1 Boil, steam or microwave potatoes until tender. Drain.
2 Meanwhile, pound garlic and salt in a mortar and pestle until smooth, or, chop the garlic and salt together on a board and use the flat side of the knife blade to press garlic into a paste.
3 When potatoes are cool enough to handle, halve and spoon out flesh. Push flesh through sieve into large bowl. Whisk in oil, juice and garlic mixture then milk. Season with salt and white pepper.

prep + cook time 40 minutes **makes** 3 cups
nutritional count per tablespoon 3.3g total fat (0.6g saturated fat); 165kJ (39 cal); 2g carbohydrate; 0.5g protein; 0.3g fibre
tip We used russet burbank potatoes, also known as idaho. You can use other floury varieties such as sebago or coliban.
serving suggestions Pitta bread and raw vegetable sticks.

Eggplant fritters with garlic yogurt

1 large eggplant (500g), cut into thick lengths
1 tablespoon coarse cooking salt
vegetable oil, for deep-frying
1 teaspoon rigani
oregano and lemon batter
½ cup (75g) plain (all-purpose) flour
⅔ cup (160ml) beer
1 tablespoon rigani
1 teaspoon finely grated lemon rind
garlic yogurt
1 cup (280g) greek-style yogurt
1 clove garlic, crushed
1 tablespoon finely chopped fresh dill

1 Place eggplant in strainer over bowl, sprinkle with salt; stand 1 hour.
2 Meanwhile, make oregano and lemon batter.
3 Make garlic yogurt.
4 Heat oil in large saucepan or wok. Rinse eggplant under cold water, pat dry with absorbent paper. Dip eggplant into batter, shake away excess. Deep-fry eggplant in batches, turning occasionally, about 5 minutes or until browned. Drain on absorbent paper.
5 Sprinkle eggplant with rigani and a little salt; serve with garlic yogurt.
oregano and lemon batter Sift flour into large bowl, gradually whisk in beer until batter is smooth. Add rigani and rind; season. Stand 1 hour.
garlic yogurt Combine ingredients in small bowl; season to taste.

prep + cook time 40 minutes (+ standing) **serves** 4
nutritional count per serving 18g total fat (4.4g saturated fat); 1295kJ (309 cal); 27g carbohydrate; 6.9g protein; 4g fibre

Yellow split pea dip

1 cup (200g) yellow split peas, rinsed, drained
3 cups (750ml) water
¼ cup finely chopped fresh flat-leaf parsley
1 clove garlic, crushed
½ teaspoon ground cumin
2 tablespoons olive oil
½ small red onion (50g), chopped finely

1 Bring peas and the water to the boil in medium saucepan. Reduce heat; simmer, uncovered, about 35 minutes or until tender. Most of the water will have evaporated; if there is water left, drain peas and reserve the liquid.
2 Process peas, parsley, garlic and cumin until smooth, adding a little of the reserved liquid if needed. Season. With motor operating, add oil; process until combined. Transfer to serving bowl. Reserve 2 teaspoons onion; stir in remaining onion.
3 Serve dip warm, sprinkled with reserved onion; drizzle with a little extra oil.

prep + cook time 45 minutes **makes** 2¼ cups
nutritional count per tablespoon 1.6g total fat (0.4g saturated fat); 151kJ (36 cal); 3.6g carbohydrate; 1.6g protein; 0.8g fibre
serving suggestions Toasted bread, pitta bread or vegetable sticks.

Taramasalata

1 largc potato (300g), chopped coarsely
90g (3 ounces) tarama
½ small white onion (40g), grated finely
¾ cup (180ml) extra light olive oil
¼ cup (60ml) white wine vinegar
1 tablespoon lemon juice

1 Boil, steam or microwave potato until tender; cool. Refrigerate until cold.
2 Mash potato in small bowl with remaining ingredients until smooth.

prep + cook time 25 minutes (+ refrigeration) **makes** 1⅔ cups
nutritional count per tablespoon 10.7g total fat (1.6g saturated fat); 472kJ (113 cal); 2.6g carbohydrate; 1.6g protein; 0.3g fibre
tips Tarama is salt-cured carp or cod roe, available in fish shops.
This recipe uses mashed potato but there are variations using bread soaked in water.
The colour of this dip can vary from beige to pink depending on the roe (commercial taramasalata is often coloured pink).

Tzatziki

500g (1 pound) yogurt
1 lebanese cucumber (130g), peeled, grated coarsely
½ teaspoon salt
1 clove garlic, crushed
1 tablespoon lemon juice
2 tablespoons finely chopped fresh mint

1 Place yogurt onto large square of double-thickness muslin. Tie ends of muslin together; hang over large bowl, or place in a sieve to drain. Refrigerate about 2 hours or until yogurt is thick; discard liquid in bowl.
2 Meanwhile, combine cucumber and salt in small bowl; stand 20 minutes. Gently squeeze excess liquid from cucumber.
3 Combine yogurt, cucumber, garlic, juice and mint in small bowl; season to taste.

prep + cook time 10 minutes (+ refrigeration) **makes** 1¾ cups
nutritional count per tablespoon 1.7g total fat (1.1g saturated fat); 125kJ (30 cal); 2.3g carbohydrate; 1.4g protein; 0.1g fibre
tips Muslin, a cotton cloth, is available in craft and cookware shops. There are many variations of this classic mezze: cucumber can be diced instead of grated, you can use dill and parsley instead of mint. It's a great side to most meat dishes.

Dolmades

2 tablespoons olive oil
2 medium brown onions (300g), chopped finely
155g (5 ounces) lean minced (ground) lamb
¾ cup (150g) white long-grain rice
2 tablespoons pine nuts
½ cup finely chopped fresh flat-leaf parsley
2 tablespoons each finely chopped fresh dill and mint
¼ cup (60ml) lemon juice
2 cups (500ml) water
500g (1 pound) preserved vine leaves
¾ cup (200g) yogurt

1 Heat oil in large saucepan; cook onion, stirring, until softened. Add lamb; cook, stirring, until browned. Stir in rice and pine nuts. Add herbs, 2 tablespoons of the juice and half the water; bring to the boil. Reduce heat; simmer, covered, 10 minutes or until water is absorbed and rice is partially cooked. Cool.
2 Rinse vine leaves in cold water. Drop leaves into a large saucepan of boiling water, in batches, for a few seconds, transfer to colander; rinse under cold water, drain well.
3 Place a vine leaf, smooth-side down on bench, trim large stem. Place a heaped teaspoon of rice mixture in centre. Fold stem end and sides over filling; roll up firmly. Line medium heavy-based saucepan with a few vine leaves; place rolls, close together, seam-side down, on leaves.
4 Pour over the remaining water; cover rolls with any remaining leaves. Place a plate on top of leaves to weigh down rolls. Cover pan tightly, bring to the boil. Reduce heat; simmer, over very low heat, 1½ hours. Remove from heat; stand, covered, about 2 hours or until liquid has been absorbed.
5 Serve dolmades with combined yogurt and remaining juice.

prep + cook time 3 hours (+ standing) **serves** 10
nutritional count per serving 7.6g total fat (1.6g saturated fat); 690kJ (165 cal); 14.9g carbohydrate; 7.7g protein; 3.2g fibre
tip Preserved vine leaves are packed in brine so should be rinsed and dried before use. Fresh leaves should be softened in boiling water for a minute until pliable, then dried.

Herbed fetta cheese

200g (6½ ounces) fetta cheese
30g (1 ounce) unsalted butter, softened
2 tablespoons finely chopped fresh oregano
1 tablespoon finely chopped fresh mint
1 teaspoon finely grated lemon rind
2 teaspoons olive oil

1 Grease 1¼-cup (310ml) dish; line with plastic wrap.
2 Process cheese and butter until smooth. Transfer to medium bowl; stir in herbs and rind. Season with pepper. Press mixture firmly into dish. Cover; refrigerate 2 hours.
3 Unmould cheese onto plate; drizzle with oil.

prep time 15 minutes (+ refrigeration) **makes** 1¼ cups
nutritional count per teaspoon 1.3g total fat (0.8g saturated fat); 60kJ (14 cal); 0g carbohydrate; 0.6g protein; 0g fibre
tip You can vary the herbs or add finely chopped olives, if you like.
serving suggestions Celery sticks and bread.

Deep-fried zucchini balls

2 medium unpeeled zucchini (240g), grated coarsely
2 teaspoons coarse cooking salt
1 small brown onion (80g), chopped finely
75g (2½ ounces) fetta cheese, crumbled
½ cup (75g) plain (all-purpose) flour
1 egg
2 tablespoons finely chopped fresh mint
1 tablespoon milk
vegetable oil, for deep-frying

1 Place zucchini in strainer; sprinkle with salt. Stand 10 minutes; squeeze excess moisture from zucchini.
2 Combine zucchini, onion, cheese, flour, egg, mint and milk in large bowl; season.
3 Heat oil in medium saucepan or wok. Deep-fry tablespoons of mixture, in batches, until browned. Drain on absorbent paper.

prep + cook time 20 minutes (+ standing) **makes** 16
nutritional count per ball 3.3g total fat (1g saturated fat); 224kJ (54 cal); 4g carbohydrate; 2g protein; 0.5g fibre
serving suggestion Yogurt for dipping.

Chickpea patties with tahini sauce

400g (12½ ounces) canned chickpeas (garbanzo beans), rinsed, drained
½ small brown onion (40g), chopped coarsely
1 egg
½ cup (50g) coarsely grated kasseri cheese
¼ cup coarsely chopped fresh oregano
1 clove garlic, crushed
1 tablespoon olive oil
½ cup (35g) stale breadcrumbs
2 tablespoons olive oil, extra

tahini sauce
2 tablespoons finely chopped fresh flat-leaf parsley
2 tablespoons tahini
2 tablespoons hot water
1 tablespoon olive oil
1 tablespoon lemon juice
1 clove garlic, crushed

1 Process chickpeas, onion, egg, cheese, oregano, garlic and olive oil until thick. Transfer to medium bowl; stir in breadcrumbs. Season to taste; stand 10 minutes.
2 Meanwhile, make tahini sauce.
3 With wet hands, shape level tablespoons of mixture into patties.
4 Heat extra oil in large frying pan; cook patties about 2 minutes each side or until browned. Drain on absorbent paper.
5 Serve patties with sauce.
tahini sauce Combine ingredients in small bowl; season to taste.

prep + cook time 30 minutes (+ standing) **makes** 22
nutritional count per patty 4.6g total fat (0.9g saturated fat); 232kJ (55 cal); 1.9g carbohydrate; 1.8g protein; 0.7g fibre

Pan-fried liver

1 medium lemon (140g)
400g (12½-ounce) thick slice veal liver
2 cloves garlic, bruised
2 tablespoons olive oil
2 teaspoons rigani

1 Using a vegetable peeler, peel rind thinly from lemon, avoiding white pith. Squeeze lemon; reserve 1 tablespoon juice.
2 Combine liver, garlic, oil, rigani and rind in shallow bowl. Cover; refrigerate 1 hour.
3 Remove liver from marinade; cut into 20 bite-sized pieces. Season.
4 Heat marinade in large frying pan over high heat; discard garlic and rind. Add liver to same pan; cook, in batches, until browned and cooked as desired. Remove from pan.
5 Return liver to pan; drizzle with reserved juice.

prep + cook time 10 minutes (+ refrigeration) **makes** 20
nutritional count per piece 3.5g total fat (0.9g saturated fat); 202kJ (48 cal); 0.2g carbohydrate; 4g protein; 0g fibre
tip Liver will toughen if overcooked, it takes only a minute or so to cook through.
serving suggestion Lemon wedges.

Pan-fried haloumi

200g (6½ ounces) haloumi cheese
2 tablespoons olive oil
2 teaspoons rigani

1 Cut cheese into slices.
2 Combine cheese, oil and rigani in shallow bowl; season with pepper. Stand 30 minutes.
3 Drain oil mixture from haloumi into large frying pan; heat oil, cook cheese until browned lightly. Serve immediately.

prep + cook time 5 minutes (+ standing) **serves** 4
nutritional count per serving 17.7g total fat (7g saturated fat); 853kJ (204 cal); 0.9g carbohydrate; 10.7g protein; 0.1g fibre
tip Fried haloumi needs to be eaten as soon as possible after cooking as it becomes tough and rubbery as it cools. It only takes a minute or so to fry, so it is best to make this dish just before serving.

Thyme and garlic marinated olives

1 medium lemon (140g)
½ cup (125ml) olive oil
2 cloves garlic, bruised
3 sprigs fresh thyme
1 bay leaf
2 cups (320g) large kalamata olives, rinsed, drained

1 Sterilise jar and lid (see tips).
2 Meanwhile, using a vegetable peeler, peel rind thinly from lemon, avoiding white pith. Combine rind, oil, garlic, thyme and bay leaf in medium saucepan over medium heat; heat until warm and garlic begins to sizzle. Add olives; cook over low heat 10 minutes.
3 Spoon hot olives into sterilised jar. Seal jar while hot.

prep + cook time 15 minutes (+ standing) **serves** 12
nutritional count per serving 7.4g total fat (1g saturated fat); 295kJ (70 cal); 0.6g carbohydrate; 0.4g protein; 0.7g fibre
tips To sterilise jars: wash the jar and lid in warm soapy water; rinse well. Place jar in large saucepan and cover with water. Bring to the boil and boil for 10 minutes. Carefully drain water from jars; transfer jar and lid to a baking tray lined with a clean tea towel. Cover with a sheet of foil and place in a low oven until dry. Use straight from the oven.
Serve olives warm if you like or store olives in refrigerator for one week.
Look for large "meaty" olives from delicatessens as they have a firm texture.

Marinated mushrooms

2 cups (500ml) white wine vinegar
½ cup (125ml) dry white wine
1 cup (250ml) water
4 bay leaves
2 tablespoons coarse cooking salt
750g (1½ pounds) baby button mushrooms
4 cloves garlic, sliced thickly
1 teaspoon black peppercorns
3 sprigs rigani
1¼ cups (310ml) extra virgin olive oil

1 Sterilise 1-litre (4-cup) jar and lid (see tips).
2 Meanwhile, combine vinegar, wine, the water, bay leaves and salt in large saucepan; heat to simmer without boiling. Add mushrooms; simmer, uncovered, 10 minutes. Drain mushrooms, reserve bay leaves; discard liquid. Spread mushrooms in single layer on absorbent paper; stand 5 minutes.
3 Spoon mushrooms into hot sterilised jar with reserved bay leaves, garlic, peppercorns and rigani. Pour hot oil over mushrooms in jar, pressing on mushrooms with back of spoon to release any trapped air, leaving 1cm (½-inch) space between mushrooms and top of jar. Seal jar while hot.

prep + cook time 25 minutes (+ standing) **makes** 4 cups
nutritional count per ¼ cup 1.9g total fat (0.3g saturated fat); 110kJ (26 cal); 0.7g carbohydrate; 1.6g protein; 0.7g fibre
tips To sterilise jars: wash the jar and lid in warm soapy water; rinse well. Place jar in large saucepan and cover with water. Bring to the boil and boil for 10 minutes. Carefully drain water from jars; transfer jar and lid to a baking tray lined with a clean tea towel. Cover with a sheet of foil and place in a low oven until dry. Use straight from oven.
Store marinated mushrooms in refrigerator for up to three months. Sometimes garlic will discolour during storage. The garlic is still edible – and harmless – if this happens.

Lamb fillo rolls

⅓ cup (80ml) olive oil
1 small brown onion (80g), chopped finely
250g (8 ounces) minced (ground) lamb
2 tablespoons dried currants
1 teaspoon ground cinnamon
½ teaspoon freshly grated nutmeg
⅓ cup (80ml) dry red wine
1 tablespoon tomato paste
2 tablespoons roasted pine nuts
2 tablespoons finely chopped fresh flat-leaf parsley
10 sheets fillo pastry

1 Heat 1 tablespoon of the oil in large frying pan; cook onion, stirring, until softened. Add lamb; cook, stirring, until browned. Stir in currants and spices. Add combined wine and paste; bring to the boil. Reduce heat; simmer, uncovered, until liquid evaporates. Cool. Stir in nuts and parsley.
2 Preheat oven to 220°C/425°F. Oil oven trays; line with baking paper.
3 Brush 1 sheet of pastry with some of the remaining oil; top with a second sheet. Cut layered sheets into four strips. Press a level tablespoon of lamb mixture in a log shape along base of one narrow edge of pastry strip, leaving 1cm (½-inch) border. Roll pastry over filling; fold in sides then roll up to make a log shape. Repeat to make 20 rolls.
4 Place rolls, seam-side down, about 2cm (¾ inch) apart, on trays. Brush rolls with a little more oil.
5 Bake rolls about 15 minutes or until browned lightly.

prep + cook time 40 minutes (+ cooling) **makes** 20
nutritional count per roll 6.6g total fat (1.3g saturated fat); 407kJ (97 cal); 5.5g carbohydrate; 3.7g protein; 0.5g fibre
tip When working with the first two sheets of pastry, cover remaining pastry with a sheet of baking paper then a damp tea towel to prevent it from drying out.

Cheese fillo triangles

1 cup (200g) cottage cheese
100g (3 ounces) fetta cheese
1 egg
2 tablespoons each finely chopped fresh oregano and flat-leaf parsley
15 sheets fillo pastry
¼ cup (60ml) olive oil

1 Preheat oven to 220°C/425°F. Oil oven trays; line with baking paper.
2 Combine cheeses, egg and herbs in medium bowl; season with pepper.
3 Brush 1 sheet of pasty with some of the oil; top with 2 more sheets, brushing each with more oil. Cut layered sheets into 3 strips lengthways. Place 1 level tablespoon of cheese mixture at one narrow edge of each pastry strip. Fold one corner of pastry diagonally over filling to form a triangle. Continue folding to end of strip, retaining triangular shape. Repeat to make 15 triangles in total.
4 Place triangles, seam-side down, on trays; brush with a little more oil. Bake triangles about 15 minutes or until browned lightly.

prep + cook time 30 minutes **makes** 15
nutritional count per triangle 6.5g total fat (2.2g saturated fat); 480kJ (115 cal); 9g carbohydrate; 5g protein; 0.4g fibre
tip When working with the first three sheets of pastry, cover remaining pastry with a sheet of baking paper then a damp tea towel to prevent it from drying out.

Spinach and cheese parcels

500g (1 pound) bunch spinach, trimmed, chopped finely
1 cup (80g) coarsely grated kefalotyri cheese
1 cup (200g) cottage cheese
2 tablespoons finely chopped fresh mint
1 egg
12 sheets fillo pastry
2 tablespoons olive oil

1 Preheat oven to 220°C/425°F. Oil oven trays, line with baking paper.
2 Cook spinach in large frying pan until wilted; drain. When cool enough to handle, squeeze excess moisture from spinach. Combine spinach in medium bowl with cheeses, mint and egg; season.
3 Brush 1 sheet of pastry with oil; top with 3 more sheets, brushing each with oil. Cut layered sheets into quarters then cut quarters in half to make 8 rectangles. Place 1 tablespoon of cheese mixture in centre of each rectangle. Fold in sides, leaving centre open. Repeat to make a total of 24 parcels.
4 Place parcels on tray; brush with oil. Bake about 15 minutes or until browned lightly.

prep + cook time 45 minutes **makes** 24
nutritional count per parcel 3.3g total fat (1.2g saturated fat); 260kJ (62 cal); 4.6g carbohydrate; 3.5g protein; 0.4g fibre
tips When working with the first four sheets of pastry, cover remaining pastry with a sheet of baking paper then a damp tea towel to prevent it drying out.
You can also make this recipe with silver beet; remove the white stalks and veins.

Deep-fried eggplant with fresh herb sauce

2 medium eggplant (600g)
2 tablespoons plain (all-purpose) flour
vegetable oil, for deep-frying
fresh herb sauce
1 cup each loosely packed fresh oregano and flat-leaf parsley leaves
⅓ cup (80ml) olive oil
2 cloves garlic, crushed
1 teaspoon finely grated lemon rind
1 tablespoon lemon juice

1 Make fresh herb sauce.
2 Cut each eggplant into 10 slices. Season flour with salt and pepper. Toss eggplant in flour, shake away excess.
3 Heat vegetable oil in medium saucepan or wok. Deep-fry eggplant, in batches, until browned and tender. Remove from pan; drain on absorbent paper.
4 Serve eggplant drizzled with sauce.
fresh herb sauce Process ingredients until smooth; season to taste.

prep + cook time 20 minutes **makes** 20 slices
nutritional count per slice 5.3g total fat (0.8g saturated fat); 230kJ (55 cal); 1.6g carbohydrate; 0.5g protein; 1g fibre
tips Store sauce in airtight container in refrigerator.
This sauce also goes well with deep-fried zucchini balls (page 36).

Grilled fetta and baby truss tomatoes

200g (6½ ounces) fetta cheese
275g (9 ounces) baby truss tomatoes
1 tablespoon olive oil
1 teaspoon rigani

1 Preheat griller (broiler).
2 Place cheese and tomatoes on oven tray. Drizzle with oil; sprinkle with rigani. Season with pepper.
3 Place under grill about 8 minutes or until cheese is browned lightly.

prep + cook time 10 minutes **serves** 4
nutritional count per serving 16g total fat (8.2g saturated fat); 796kJ (190 cal); 1.8g carbohydrate; 9.4g protein; 0.9g fibre
serving suggestion Thinly sliced toasted bread stick.

Beetroot salad

500g (1 pound) bunch baby beetroot (beets)
2 tablespoons olive oil
1 tablespoon red wine vinegar
1 tablespoon finely chopped fresh flat-leaf parsley
1 teaspoon finely chopped fresh dill
1 clove garlic, crushed

1 Discard leaves from beetroot; reserve stems. Wash beetroot and stems. Place beetroots in medium saucepan; cover with water. Bring to the boil; simmer, covered, about 30 minutes or until tender. Add stems 5 minutes before end of cooking time. Drain.
2 When beetroots are cool enough to handle, use disposable gloves to gently slip off skin from beetroots; discard skins. Slice beetroots and stems. Combine beetroots and stems in shallow bowl with combined remaining ingredients; season to taste.

prep + cook time 40 minutes (+ cooling) **serves** 4
nutritional count per serving 4.6g total fat (0.7g saturated fat); 260kJ (62 cal); 4.3g carbohydrate; 1.0g protein; 2g fibre
tip Use disposable gloves when handling beetroot to prevent your hands becoming stained.

Fried lamb meatballs

300g (10 ounces) minced (ground) lamb
1 small brown onion (80g), chopped finely
60g (2 ounces) fetta cheese, crumbled
½ cup (35g) stale breadcrumbs
1 egg
2 tablespoons finely chopped fresh mint
2 tablespoons olive oil

1 Combine lamb, onion, cheese, breadcrumbs, egg and mint in medium bowl; season. Roll level tablespoons of mixture into balls.
2 Heat oil in large frying pan; cook balls, in batches, until browned and cooked through. Drain on absorbent paper.

prep + cook time 20 minutes **makes** 24
nutritional count per meatball 4g total fat (1.4g saturated fat); 225kJ (54 cal); 0.8g carbohydrate; 3.6g protein; 0.1g fibre
tips To shape the meatballs well, it's important to chop the onion finely. The secret to round meatballs is to make a circular movement with the pan to roll the meatballs around the pan while they cook.
serving suggestion Tzatziki (page 31).

Deep-fried baby calamari

500g (1 pound) baby calamari, cleaned
⅓ cup (50g) plain (all-purpose) flour
vegetable oil, for deep-frying
2 teaspoons rigani

1 Slice calamari into thin rings. Season flour with salt and pepper.
2 Heat oil in medium saucepan or wok. Toss calamari in flour mixture; shake away excess. Deep-fry calamari, in batches, until browned lightly and tender. Drain on absorbent paper. Sprinkle with rigani; serve with a squeeze of lemon juice.

prep + cook time 15 minutes **serves** 4
nutritional count per serving 4g total fat (0.6g saturated fat); 425kJ (100 cal); 6.4g carbohydrate; 9.9g protein; 0.4g fibre
tips Don't overcook the calamari or it will toughen. It should take about 30 seconds to cook one small batch at a time. Reheat the oil before frying the next batch of calamari. Ask the fishmonger to clean the calamari for you.
serving suggestion Lemon wedges.

Marinated sardines

20 small butterflied sardines (550g)
5 flat-leaf parsley stems
½ cup (125ml) lemon juice
¼ cup (60ml) olive oil
2 teaspoons coarse cooking salt
1 tablespoon lemon juice, extra
1 tablespoon olive oil, extra
½ small red onion (50g), sliced thinly
1 tablespoon coarsely chopped fresh flat-leaf parsley

1 Place sardines, skin-side down, in single layer in glass or ceramic dish; top with parsley stems.
2 Combine juice, oil and salt in small bowl; drizzle over sardines. Cover; refrigerate overnight or until sardine flesh turns white.
3 Discard parsley stems; place drained sardines on platter. Drizzle with combined extra juice and extra oil; season. Sprinkle with onion and chopped parsley.

prep time 15 minutes (+ refrigeration) **makes** 20
nutritional count per sardine 2.8g total fat (0.6g saturated fat); 204kJ (49 cal); 0.2g carbohydrate; 5.6g protein; 0.1g fibre
tips Ask your fishmonger to butterfly the sardines.
It is correct that the sardines are not cooked in this recipe.

Prawn and haloumi kebabs

90g (3 ounces) haloumi cheese
18 uncooked small prawns (shrimp) (450g), shelled, deveined
2 teaspoons rigani
2 tablespoons olive oil
6 bay leaves, halved

1 Cut cheese into 12 bite-sized pieces. Combine cheese, prawns, rigani and oil in shallow bowl. Thread prawns, bay leaves and cheese alternately onto 6 small skewers; season with pepper.
2 Cook skewers on heated grill plate (or grill or barbecue or grill pan) over medium-high heat until prawns are cooked through.

prep + cook time 20 minutes **makes** 6
nutritional count per skewer 8.9g total fat (2.7g saturated fat); 520kJ (124 cal); 0.3g carbohydrate; 10.9g protein; 0.1g fibre
tip Soak bamboo skewers in water for 1 hour before using to prevent them scorching during cooking.
serving suggestions Lemon wedges and bread.

Zucchini and beef sfougato

1 large potato (300g), unpeeled
3 medium zucchini (360g), grated coarsely
2 teaspoons coarse cooking salt
1 tablespoon olive oil
300g (10 ounces) minced (ground) beef
4 green onions (scallions), chopped finely
6 eggs
2 tablespoons finely chopped fresh mint
1 tablespoon finely chopped fresh dill
1 cup (125g) coarsely grated kasseri cheese
1 cup (80g) coarsely grated kefalotyri cheese

1 Boil, steam or microwave whole potato until tender. Cool; peel, then grate coarsely.
2 Place zucchini in colander; sprinkle with salt. Stand 10 minutes; squeeze excess moisture from zucchini.
3 Meanwhile, preheat oven to 200°C/400°F. Oil 20cm x 30cm (8-inch x 12-inch) slice pan; line with baking paper, extending paper 5cm (2 inches) over long sides.
4 Heat half the oil in large frying pan; cook beef and onion, stirring, until beef is browned. Transfer beef mixture to large bowl.
5 Heat remaining oil in same pan; cook zucchini, stirring, until softened. Add to beef mixture. Stir in potato, eggs, herbs and half the cheeses; season. Spoon mixture into pan; sprinkle with remaining cheese.
6 Bake about 30 minutes or until set and browned lightly. Stand in pan 5 minutes before cutting.

prep + cook time 1 hour (+ standing) **makes** 30 pieces
nutritional count per piece 4.3g total fat (2g saturated fat); 278kJ (66 cal); 1.5g carbohydrate; 5.5g protein; 0.3g fibre
tip You can serve this dish warm or at room temperature. It's a great recipe for picnics or lunch boxes.

Tomato and fetta toasts

200g (6½ ounces) baguette (french bread stick)
2 tablespoons olive oil
1 clove garlic, peeled, halved
3 small ripe tomatoes (270g), chopped finely
50g (1½ ounces) fetta cheese, crumbled
1 tablespoon fresh oregano leaves

1 Preheat oven to 170°C/340°F.
2 Cut bread on the diagonal into four thick slices; split slices. Brush bread with half the oil. Place on oven tray. Toast in oven about 20 minutes, turning bread halfway, or until crisp. Rub toasts with garlic.
3 Season tomato; spoon onto toasts. Stand 20 minutes.
4 Top tomato with cheese; drizzle with remaining oil. Sprinkle with oregano.

prep + cook time 35 minutes (+ standing) **makes** 8
nutritional count per toast 6.6g total fat (1.8g saturated fat); 530kJ (126 cal); 12.6g carbohydrate; 4.2g protein; 1.2g fibre
tip This mezze is very simple. Success lies in the quality of the ingredients: choose ripe tomatoes, good bread and a quality oil.

Haloumi and asparagus bites

340g (11 ounces) asparagus, trimmed
250g (8 ounces) haloumi cheese
lemony dressing
1 tablespoon rinsed, drained baby capers, chopped finely
1 tablespoon olive oil
2 teaspoons finely grated lemon rind
1 tablespoon lemon juice
½ teaspoon white sugar

1 Make lemony dressing.
2 Cut asparagus into bite-sized pieces. Boil, steam or microwave until just tender; rinse under cold water, drain.
3 Cut cheese into bite-sized pieces. Thread one piece of asparagus, one piece of cheese, then another piece of asparagus close together onto each toothpick.
4 Cook bites in large oiled frying pan over high heat about 30 seconds each side or until browned lightly.
5 Serve bites immediately, drizzled with dressing.
lemony dressing Place ingredients in screw-top jar; shake well.

prep + cook time 55 minutes **makes** 40
nutritional count per bite 1.5g total fat (0.8g saturated fat); 88kJ (21 cal); 0.3g carbohydrate; 1.5g protein; 0.1g fibre

Broad bean patties with minted yogurt

½ cup (100g) green split peas
500g (1 pound) frozen broad (fava) beans
1 medium brown onion (150g), chopped finely
2 cloves garlic, crushed
⅓ cup (50g) wholemeal plain (all-purpose) flour
¼ cup (25g) packaged breadcrumbs
1 egg
cooking-oil spray
minted yogurt
⅔ cup (190g) low-fat yogurt
¼ cup finely chopped fresh mint
1 teaspoon finely grated lime rind
2 tablespoons lime juice

1 Place peas in medium saucepan of boiling water; return to the boil. Reduce heat; simmer until tender. Drain.
2 Meanwhile, place beans in medium saucepan of boiling water; return to the boil. Drain. Cool in iced water; drain. Discard skin. Mash beans and peas together in large bowl; cool.
3 Stir onion, garlic, flour, breadcrumbs and egg into bean mixture; season to taste. Using hands, shape mixture into eight patties; place on baking-paper-lined tray. Refrigerate 30 minutes.
4 Meanwhile, make minted yogurt.
5 Lightly spray heated large frying pan with oil; cook patties, in batches, until browned and heated through. Remove from pan.
6 Serve patties with minted yogurt.
minted yogurt Combine ingredients in small bowl; season to taste.

prep + cook time 40 minutes (+ refrigeration) **serves** 4
nutritional count per serving 3.6g total fat (0.7g saturated fat); 1087kJ (260 cal); 30.7g carbohydrate; 19.8g protein; 11.5g fibre

Pickled vegetables

2 medium red capsicums (bell peppers) (400g)
1 litre (4 cups) white vinegar
2 cups (500ml) water
6 black peppercorns
1 bay leaf
1 tablespoon sea salt flakes
1 small eggplant (230g), quartered lengthways, cut into 1cm (½-inch) slices
½ small cauliflower (200g), cut into florets
2 medium carrots (240g), sliced thinly diagonally
2 stalks celery (300g), trimmed, sliced thickly diagonally
2 tablespoons finely chopped fresh flat-leaf parsley
2 teaspoons finely chopped fresh thyme
2 cups (500ml) olive oil
2 cloves garlic, sliced thinly

1 Preheat oven to 200°C/400°F. Sterilise 1.5-litre (6-cup) jar and lid (see tip).
2 Quarter capsicums; discard seeds and membranes. Roast capsicum, skin-side up, until skin blisters and blackens. Cover capsicum with plastic or paper for 5 minutes; peel away skin then slice thickly.
3 Meanwhile, combine vinegar, the water, peppercorns, bay leaf and half the salt in large saucepan; heat without boiling. Add eggplant, cauliflower, carrot and celery; bring to the boil. Reduce heat; simmer, uncovered, 5 minutes or until vegetables are tender. Drain vegetables; discard liquid.
4 Combine hot vegetables, capsicum, herbs and remaining salt in large heatproof bowl. Spoon vegetable mixture into sterilised jar.
5 Heat oil and garlic in small saucepan, strain into large heatproof jug; discard garlic. Carefully pour hot oil over vegetables to cover, leaving a 1cm (½-inch) space between vegetables and top of jar. Seal while hot.

prep + cook time 1 hour **makes** 6 cups
nutritional count per ¼ cup 19.1g total fat (2.7g saturated fat); 748kJ (179 cal); 1.6g carbohydrate; 0.7g protein; 1g fibre
tip To sterilise jars: wash the jar and lid in warm soapy water; rinse well. Place jar in large saucepan and cover with water. Bring to the boil and boil for 10 minutes. Carefully drain water from jars; transfer jar and lid to a baking tray lined with a clean tea towel. Cover with a sheet of foil and place in a low oven until dry. Use straight from the oven.

Braised artichokes with crunchy almond topping

6 large globe artichokes (2.4kg)
4 bay leaves
4 cloves garlic
1 litre (4 cups) chicken stock
crunchy almond topping
¾ cup (50g) fresh breadcrumbs
⅓ cup (25g) flaked almonds
½ cup (60g) seeded green olives, chopped finely
¼ cup (60ml) olive oil
2 tablespoons finely chopped fresh flat-leaf parsley
1 tablespoon finely grated lemon rind
2 tablespoons lemon juice

1 Preheat oven to 200°C/400°F.
2 Prepare artichokes by snapping off tough outer leaves and peeling stems. Trim stems to 5cm (2 inches). Cut 2cm (¾ inch) off top of artichokes to reveal chokes. Cut artichokes in half from top to bottom, then scoop out and discard furry chokes from the centres. As you finish preparing each artichoke, place it in a large bowl of water containing the juice of about half a lemon (this stops any discolouration while you are preparing the next one).
3 Drain artichokes. Combine artichokes, bay leaves, garlic and stock in small baking dish, ensuring artichokes are covered with stock. Bake, covered, about 45 minutes or until artichokes are tender.
4 Meanwhile, make crunchy almond topping.
5 Drain artichokes; discard liquid. Serve artichokes hot or at room temperature sprinkled with topping.
crunchy almond topping Combine breadcrumbs and nuts on oven tray; roast 5 minutes or until golden. Cool 5 minutes. Combine breadcrumb mixture with remaining ingredients in small bowl.

prep + cook time 1 hour 40 minutes **serves** 6
nutritional count per serving 13.1g total fat (1.9g saturated fat); 928kJ (222 cal); 13.1g carbohydrate; 11.6g protein; 3.3g fibre
tip Raw artichokes can stain your hands, so wear plastic gloves when preparing them.

Grilled eggplant with marjoram vinaigrette

1 large eggplant (500g), sliced into 5mm (¼-inch) rounds
¾ cup (180ml) olive oil
1 small red onion (100g), sliced thinly
¼ cup (60ml) sherry vinegar
2 teaspoons caster (superfine) sugar
2 tablespoons finely chopped fresh marjoram

1 Preheat oven to 200°C/400°F. Line baking trays with baking paper.
2 Brush both sides of eggplant slices with ¼ cup of the oil; place slices, in single layer, on trays.
3 Bake about 25 minutes, turning halfway through, until browned.
4 Meanwhile, combine remaining oil with remaining ingredients in small bowl.
5 Spoon vinaigrette over eggplant. Serve warm or at room temperature.

prep + cook time 50 minutes **serves** 6
nutritional count per serving 28.3g total fat (4g saturated fat); 1112kJ (278 cal); 4.6g carbohydrate; 1.2g protein; 2.2g fibre
tip Marjoram has a sweet pine and citrus flavour. You can use fresh oregano instead.
serving suggestion Crusty bread.

Barbecued seafood platter

16 uncooked medium king prawns (shrimp) (720g)
1 tablespoon finely chopped fresh oregano
1 teaspoon finely grated lemon rind
½ teaspoon dried chilli flakes
1 clove garlic, crushed
2 tablespoons olive oil
8 slices prosciutto (120g)
8 butterflied sardines (240g)
300g (9½ ounces) baby octopus, quartered
200g (6½ ounces) squid hoods, sliced into rings
2 tablespoons balsamic vinegar
¼ cup coarsely chopped fresh flat-leaf parsley
500g (1 pound) small black mussels
¼ cup (60ml) lemon juice
1 medium tomato (150g), seeded, chopped finely

1 Remove and discard prawn heads, leaving shells intact. Cut prawns lengthways, three-quarters of the way through, leaving 1cm (½ inch) before the tail; press down on prawns to flatten.
2 Combine prawns, oregano, rind, chilli, garlic and half the oil in medium bowl. Cover; refrigerate 1 hour.
3 Wrap a prosciutto slice firmly around each sardine.
4 Cook octopus and squid on heated oiled grill plate (or grill or barbecue) until tender. Combine octopus and squid in medium heatproof bowl with remaining oil, vinegar and 2 tablespoons of the parsley. Cover to keep warm.
5 Cook prawns and sardines on same heated oiled grill plate.
6 Meanwhile, cook mussels, covered, on heated oiled flat plate about 5 minutes or until mussels open (discard any that do not). Place mussels in medium heatproof bowl; drizzle with juice, sprinkle with tomato and remaining parsley.
7 Serve seafood with lemon wedges.

prep + cook time 1 hour (+ refrigeration) **serves** 8
nutritional count per serving 8.7g total fat (1.7g saturated fat); 836kJ (200 cal); 1.3g carbohydrate; 28.5g protein; 0.4g fibre

Barbecued baby octopus

1kg (2 pounds) baby octopus
⅓ cup (80ml) lemon juice
⅓ cup (80ml) olive oil
2 cloves garlic, crushed
2 teaspoons rigani

1 Clean octopus; discard eyes and beaks.
2 Combine octopus with remaining ingredients in medium bowl. Cover; refrigerate 3 hours or overnight.
3 Drain octopus; discard marinade. Cook octopus on heated oiled grill plate (or grill or barbecue) until tender.

prep + cook time 25 minutes (+ refrigeration) **serves** 6
nutritional count per serving 13.4g total fat (1.7g saturated fat); 982kJ (235 cal); 1g carbohydrate; 27.6g protein; 0.2g fibre
tips Ask the fishmonger to clean the baby octopus for you. Don't overcook baby octopus or it will be tough. It's ready as soon as it changes colour.
serving suggestions Lemon wedges and tzatziki (page 31).

Saganaki prawns

1 tablespoon olive oil
1 medium white onion (150g), chopped finely
4 cloves garlic, crushed
410g (13 ounces) canned crushed tomatoes
¾ cup (180ml) dry white wine
2kg (4 pounds) uncooked medium king prawns (shrimp)
¼ cup each coarsely chopped fresh flat-leaf parsley and fresh oregano
200g (6½ ounces) fetta cheese, crumbled

1 Heat oil in large frying pan; cook onion and garlic, stirring, until onion softens. Add tomatoes and wine; bring to the boil. Reduce heat; simmer, covered, 10 minutes, stirring occasionally.
2 Meanwhile, shell and devein prawns, leaving tails intact.
3 Add prawns and herbs to tomato mixture; simmer, covered, 10 minutes, stirring occasionally.
4 Meanwhile, preheat grill (broiler).
5 Sprinkle cheese over prawn mixture; place under grill until cheese browns lightly.

prep + cook time 45 minutes **serves** 4
nutritional count per serving 18g total fat (8.6g saturated fat); 1956kJ (468 cal); 5.8g carbohydrate; 61.8g protein; 2.4g fibre
tip "Saganaki", meaning little frying pan in Greek, refers today to a number of dishes cooked in a single frying pan.

Pickled octopus

1.5kg (3-pound) large octopus
¾ cup (180ml) extra virgin olive oil
½ cup (125ml) white wine vinegar
1 clove garlic, crushed
2 tablespoons coarsely chopped fresh flat-leaf parsley

1 Clean octopus; discard eyes and beak. Place octopus in large saucepan without any liquid. Cook, covered, over low heat about 1 hour or until octopus is tender. (The octopus will cook in its own juices but, if necessary, add a little water if the juices evaporate.) Cool octopus in pan until cool enough to handle. Rinse octopus under cold water, remove skin, leaving tentacles intact.
2 Cut octopus into bite-sized pieces. Place octopus in medium bowl with oil, vinegar and garlic; toss gently to combine. Season to taste. Cover; refrigerate overnight.
3 Serve pickled octopus sprinkled with parsley.

prep + cook time 1 hour 10 minutes (+ cooling & refrigeration)
serves 8
nutritional count per serving 21.8g total fat (2.9g saturated fat); 1333kJ (319 cal); 0.2g carbohydrate; 30.8g protein; 0.1g fibre
tips We used a large octopus in this recipe, but you could also use baby octopus. Ask the fishmonger to clean the octopus.
Recipe can be made up to 4 days ahead; store, covered, in the refrigerator.
serving suggestion Lemon wedges.

Octopus salad with grilled tomatoes

4 large egg tomatoes (360g), halved
1 tablespoon fresh thyme leaves
2 tablespoons olive oil
1kg (2 pounds) cleaned baby octopus
270g (8½ ounces) bottled char-grilled red capsicum (bell pepper), drained, sliced thinly
1 medium oak leaf lettuce, torn
2 tablespoons rinsed, drained capers, chopped coarsely
2 lebanese cucumbers (260g), chopped coarsely
½ cup (75g) seeded black olives, chopped coarsely
½ cup coarsely chopped fresh flat-leaf parsley
¼ cup (60ml) lemon juice
1 clove garlic, crushed

1 Place tomato, thyme and half the oil in medium bowl; toss gently to combine. Cook on heated oiled flat plate, uncovered, until just softened and browned lightly.
2 Meanwhile, cook octopus on heated oiled grill plate (or grill or barbecue), brushing with remaining oil, until tender.
3 Place octopus in large bowl with remaining ingredients; toss gently to combine. Serve salad with grilled tomato.

prep + cook time 20 minutes **serves** 4
nutritional count per serving 14.4g total fat (1.6g saturated fat); 1455kJ (348 cal); 9.7g carbohydrate; 43g protein; 3.1g fibre

Artichoke spinach dip

340g (11 ounces) jar marinated artichokes, rinsed, drained
250g (8 ounces) frozen chopped spinach, thawed
½ cup (120g) sour cream
¼ cup (75g) mayonnaise
¾ cup (60g) coarsely grated kefalotyri cheese
1 clove garlic, crushed

1 Preheat oven to 200°C/400°F.
2 Chop artichokes coarsely. Combine artichokes with remaining ingredients in medium bowl. Transfer mixture to 2-cup (500ml) ovenproof dish.
3 Cook dip, covered, 20 minutes.

prep + cook time 30 minutes **makes** 2 cups
nutritional count per tablespoon 2.7g total fat (1.3g saturated fat); 130kJ (31 cal); 0.7g carbohydrate; 1.1g protein; 0.4g fibre

Roasted fennel dip

4 baby fennel bulbs with fronds (520g)
2 cloves garlic, unpeeled
1 tablespoon olive oil
1 cup (240g) sour cream

1 Preheat oven to 200°C/400°F.
2 Halve fennel lengthways; remove and discard cores. Reserve 2 teaspoons coarsely chopped fennel fronds.
3 Combine fennel with garlic and oil in small baking dish; roast about 30 minutes or until fennel is tender. Cool.
4 Peel garlic; blend or process fennel, garlic and sour cream until smooth. Serve dip sprinkled with reserved fennel fronds.

prep + cook time 45 minutes (+ cooling) **makes** 1 ½ cups
nutritional count per tablespoon 6.4g total fat (3.6g saturated fat); 268kJ (64 cal); 0.8g carbohydrate; 0.4g protein; 0.4g fibre

Beetroot and yogurt dip

500g (1 pound) beetroot (beets)
½ cup (140g) yogurt
1 clove garlic, crushed
2 tablespoons lemon juice
2 tablespoons coarsely chopped fresh mint

1 Preheat oven to 200°C/400°F. Oil oven tray, line with baking paper.
2 Wash beetroot well; discard leaves. Place unpeeled beetroot on oven tray. Roast about 1 hour or until tender. When beetroot are cool enough to handle, peel and chop coarsely; cool.
3 Process beetroot. Add remaining ingredients; process until smooth.

prep + cook time 1 hour 30 minutes (+ cooling) **makes** 1⅓ cups
nutritional count per tablespoon 0.8g total fat (0.4g saturated fat); 100kJ (24 cal); 3.2g carbohydrate; 1.2g protein; 0.8g fibre
tips Use disposable gloves when handling beetroot to prevent your hands becoming stained. Beetroot dip can be made up to two days ahead; store, covered, in the refrigerator.
serving suggestion Torn pieces of heated pitta bread.

Eggplant dip

2 medium eggplants (600g)
¼ cup (60ml) olive oil
2 tablespoons finely chopped fresh flat-leaf parsley
½ small red onion (50g), chopped finely
1 medium ripe tomato (150g), chopped finely
1 tablespoon lemon juice

1 Stab eggplants all over with a fork. Grill eggplants over low flame of gas or barbecue until charred and tender. When eggplants are cool enough to handle, pull away and discard skin.
2 Coarsely chop eggplant flesh; combine with oil in large bowl. Stir in remaining ingredients; season to taste.

prep + cook time 25 minutes (+ cooling) **makes** 2½ cups
nutritional count per tablespoon 1.9g total fat (0.3g saturated fat); 84kJ (20 cal); 0.6g carbohydrate; 0.3g protein; 0.5g fibre
tip There are many versions of this dish. Grilling the eggplant over a flame gives it a smoky flavour. If you find it too messy, you can also roast them in the oven or in a covered barbecue.
serving suggestion Pitta bread.

Vegetable and haloumi skewers

180g (5½ ounces) haloumi cheese
1 small red capsicum (bell pepper) (150g)
1 large zucchini (150g)
½ cup (150g) mayonnaise
1 tablespoon lemon juice
2 teaspoons harissa

1 Cut cheese, capsicum and zucchini each into 16 bite-sized pieces.
2 Thread cheese, capsicum and zucchini onto 16 small bamboo skewers or strong toothpicks. Cook skewers on heated oiled grill plate (or grill or barbecue) until tender.
3 Meanwhile, combine remaining ingredients in small bowl; season to taste.
4 Serve skewers immediately with lemon and harissa mayonnaise.

prep + cook time 35 minutes **makes** 16
nutritional count per skewer 26.2g total fat (4g saturated fat); 1296kJ (310 cal); 15.6g carbohydrate; 3.4g protein; 0.7g fibre
tip Soak bamboo skewers in cold water for at least an hour before using to prevent them from scorching during cooking.

Lamb kebabs with yogurt and pitta bread

500g (1 pound) minced (ground) lamb
1 egg
1 small brown onion (80g), chopped finely
2 tablespoons finely chopped fresh flat-leaf parsley
1 clove garlic, crushed
2 teaspoons each ground cinnamon and sweet paprika
½ teaspoon cayenne pepper
½ cup (140g) yogurt

1 Combine lamb, egg, onion, parsley, garlic and spices in medium bowl. Roll mixture into 16 sausage shapes.
2 Thread sausage shapes onto 16 small bamboo skewers or strong toothpicks; flatten slightly. Cook on heated oiled grill plate (or grill or barbecue) until browned and cooked through.
3 Serve kebabs with yogurt.

prep + cook time 30 minutes **makes** 16
nutritional count per skewer 2.7g total fat (1.2g saturated fat); 251kJ (60 cal); 1.4g carbohydrate; 7.3g protein; 0.1g fibre
tip Soak bamboo skewers in cold water for at least an hour before using to prevent them from scorching during cooking.
serving suggestions Lemon wedges and pitta bread.

Mini chicken souvlakia

1kg (2 pounds) chicken thigh fillets
2 tablespoons olive oil
2 tablespoons lemon juice
⅓ cup finely chopped fresh mint
2 cloves garlic, crushed
1½ teaspoons smoked paprika

1 Trim any fat from chicken; cut into 2cm (¾-inch) thick strips. Combine chicken with remaining ingredients in medium bowl. Thread chicken onto 20 bamboo skewers. Cover; refrigerate 3 hours or overnight.
2 Cook skewers on heated oiled grill plate (or grill or barbecue) until browned and cooked through.

prep + cook time 35 minutes (+ refrigeration) **makes** 20
nutritional count per skewer 5.4g total fat (1.4g saturated fat); 364kJ (87 cal); 0.1g carbohydrate; 9.4g protein; 0.1g fibre
tips Soak bamboo skewers in cold water for at least an hour before using to prevent them from scorching during cooking.
For optimum flavour, marinate the chicken overnight.
serving suggestion Lemon wedges.

Roasted beetroot and fetta pizza

2 tablespoons olive oil
1kg (2 pounds) raw baby beetroots (beets), trimmed, peeled, quartered
4 cloves garlic, crushed
2 teaspoons fresh thyme leaves
4 large pitta breads (320g)
1 cup (260g) bottled tomato pasta sauce
200g (6½ ounces) fetta cheese, crumbled
20g (¾ ounce) baby rocket (arugula) leaves

1 Preheat oven to 200°C/400°F.
2 Combine oil, beetroot, garlic and thyme in medium shallow baking dish. Roast about 20 minutes or until beetroot is tender.
3 Place pitta on oven trays; spread with pasta sauce. Divide beetroot mixture among pitta; sprinkle with cheese.
4 Cook pizzas about 10 minutes or until pitta bases are crisp.
5 Sprinkle pizzas with rocket. Serve cut into wedges.

prep + cook time 45 minutes **makes** 4
nutritional count per pizza 23.5g total fat (9.3g saturated fat); 2516kJ (602 cal); 70.4g carbohydrate; 22.5g protein; 12g fibre
tips Canned baby beetroots won't work as well as roasted fresh ones. Make individual pizzas by using pocket pitta bread.

Fetta and artichoke pizzetta

1 small pizza base (112g)
50g (1½ ounces) fetta cheese, crumbled
1 teaspoon olive oil
1 marinated artichoke (70g), sliced thinly
1 tablespoon fresh oregano leaves
2 teaspoons lemon juice

1 Preheat oven to 220°C/425°F. Place pizza base on oven tray.
2 Combine 1 tablespoon of the cheese with oil. Spread pizza base with cheese paste; top with artichoke then sprinkle with remaining cheese.
3 Bake about 8 minutes.
4 Serve pizzetta sprinkled with oregano and juice.

prep + cook time 15 minutes **makes** 1
nutritional count per pizzetta 22g total fat (9.2g saturated fat); 2223kJ (532 cal); 60.8g carbohydrate; 20.3g protein; 4.2g fibre
tip Double or quadruple the recipe depending on how many you wish to serve.

Lamb and tomato pide

1 tablespoon olive oil
1 medium brown onion (150g), chopped finely
1 clove garlic, crushed
300g (9½ ounces) minced (ground) lamb
1 teaspoon each ground cinnamon, cumin and smoked paprika
½ teaspoon cayenne pepper
1 tablespoon coarsely chopped fresh coriander (cilantro)
1 medium tomato (150g), diced

basic pide dough
7g (¼ ounce) yeast
1 teaspoon sugar
⅔ cup (160ml) warm water
2 tablespoons warm milk
2 cups (300g) plain (all-purpose) flour
1 tablespoon olive oil
1 teaspoon salt

1 Make basic pide dough.
2 Preheat oven to 240°C/450°F.
3 Heat oil in frying pan; cook onion and garlic, stirring, until tender. Add lamb and spices; cook until lamb is browned. Stir in coriander; cool.
4 Divide dough into three; roll each to 12cm x 30cm (4¾-inch x 12-inch) rectangle. Spread lamb filling across centre of each piece, leaving 2cm (¾-inch) border. Brush edges with water; fold and press around dough. Fold corners to make oval shape.
5 Heat oven trays 3 minutes, place pide on trays; bake 10 minutes. Sprinkle with tomato; bake 5 minutes. Cut each pide into slices.
basic pide dough Combine yeast, sugar, the water and milk in jug; stand in warm place until frothy. Place ½ cup of the flour in bowl; whisk in yeast mixture. Cover; stand in warm place 1 hour. Stir in remaining flour, oil and salt. Knead dough on floured surface until smooth. Place in oiled bowl, cover; stand in warm place 1 hour.

prep + cook time 1 hour (+ standing) **serves** 8
nutritional count per serving 10.5g total fat (2.4g saturated fat); 1087kJ (260 cal); 27.5g carbohydrate; 12.6g protein; 2.2g fibre

Spinach and fetta pide

300g (9½ ounces) spinach, trimmed
100g (3 ounces) fetta cheese, crumbled
90g (3 ounces) coarsely grated haloumi cheese
basic pide dough
7g (¼ ounce) yeast
1 teaspoon sugar
⅔ cup (160ml) warm water
2 tablespoons warm milk
2 cups (300g) plain (all-purpose) flour
1 tablespoon olive oil
1 teaspoon salt

1 Make basic pide dough.
2 Preheat oven to 240°C/450°F.
3 Boil, steam or microwave spinach until just wilted; drain. When cool enough to handle, squeeze excess liquid from spinach; shred finely. Combine spinach and cheeses in medium bowl.
4 Divide dough into three; roll each to 12cm x 30cm (4¾-inch x 12-inch) rectangle. Spread spinach filling across centre of each piece, leaving 2cm (¾-inch) border. Brush edges with water; fold and press around dough. Fold corners to make oval shape.
5 Heat oven trays 3 minutes, place pide on trays; bake 15 minutes. Cut each pide into eight slices.
basic pide dough Combine yeast, sugar, the water and milk in jug; stand in warm place until frothy. Place ½ cup of the flour in bowl; whisk in yeast mixture. Cover; stand in warm place 1 hour. Stir in remaining flour, oil and salt. Knead dough on floured surface until smooth. Place in oiled bowl, cover; stand in warm place 1 hour.

prep + cook time 55 minutes (+ standing) **serves** 8
nutritional count per serving 10.5g total fat (4g saturated fat); 1028kJ (246 cal); 26.5g carbohydrate; 9.9g protein; 2.6g fibre

Pumpkin and fetta pide

200g (6½ ounces) pumpkin, chopped coarsely
100g (3 ounces) fetta cheese, diced
½ cup (50g) coarsely grated kasseri cheese
1 tablespoon finely chopped fresh flat-leaf parsley

basic pide dough

7g (¼ ounce) yeast
1 teaspoon sugar
⅔ cup (160ml) warm water
2 tablespoons warm milk
2 cups (300g) plain (all-purpose) flour
1 tablespoon olive oil
1 teaspoon salt

1 Make basic pide dough.

2 Preheat oven to 240°C/450°F.

3 Boil, steam or microwave pumpkin until tender; drain, cool. Combine with cheeses in medium bowl.

4 Divide dough into three; roll each to 12cm x 30cm (4¾-inch x 12-inch) rectangle. Spread pumpkin filling across centre of each piece, leaving 2cm (¾-inch) border. Brush edges with water; fold and press around dough. Fold corners to make oval shape.

5 Heat oven trays 3 minutes, place pide on trays; bake 15 minutes. Sprinkle pide with parsley. Cut each pide into eight slices.

basic pide dough Combine yeast, sugar, the water and milk in jug; stand in warm place until frothy. Place ½ cup of the flour in bowl; whisk in yeast mixture. Cover; stand in warm place 1 hour. Stir in remaining flour, oil and salt. Knead dough on floured surface until smooth. Place in oiled bowl, cover; stand in warm place 1 hour.

prep + cook time 1 hour (+ standing) **serves** 8
nutritional count per serving 10.2g total fat (3.9g saturated fat); 1020kJ (244 cal); 26.7g carbohydrate; 9.1g protein; 1.9g fibre

Eggplant, haloumi and rocket pizza

1½ cups (225g) plain (all-purpose) flour
1 teaspoon dried yeast
½ teaspoon salt
¾ cup (180ml) warm water
2 tablespoons olive oil
2 cloves garlic, crushed
¾ cup (195g) bottled tomato pasta sauce
2 small red onions (200g), cut into wedges
1 small eggplant (230g), sliced thinly
250g (8 ounces) haloumi cheese, sliced thinly
¼ cup firmly packed fresh oregano leaves
60g (2 ounces) rocket (arugula) leaves

1 Combine flour, yeast and salt in medium bowl; gradually stir in the water and half the oil. Mix to a soft, sticky dough; turn onto floured surface, knead about 10 minutes or until smooth and elastic. Shape dough into ball; place in large oiled bowl. Cover; stand in warm place about 1 hour or until dough doubles in size.
2 Preheat oven to 230°C/435°F. Oil two oven trays.
3 Punch down dough; knead until smooth. Divide dough in half; roll each half on floured surface into two 23cm x 33cm (9-inch x 13-inch) rectangles. Place dough on trays; prick with fork, spread with combined garlic and pasta sauce. Stand in warm place 10 minutes.
4 Meanwhile, combine onion, eggplant and remaining oil in large bowl. Cook vegetables, in batches, on heated grill plate (or grill or barbecue) until browned on both sides.
5 Top pizza bases with grilled vegetables, cheese and oregano. Bake about 15 minutes or until crust is golden brown. Serve topped with rocket.

prep + cook time 40 minutes (+ standing) **serves** 4
nutritional count per serving 21.2g total fat (8.3g saturated fat); 2065kJ (494 cal); 50.9g carbohydrate; 22.1g protein; 5.6g fibre
tip Making your own pizza bases is not difficult and it's rewarding, but, if time is short, buy the bases and use the topping ingredients we've suggested.

Beef and fig cigars

20g (3/4 ounce) butter
1 medium brown onion (150g), chopped finely
1/2 teaspoon ground cinnamon
2 cloves garlic, crushed
250g (8 ounces) minced (ground) beef
3/4 cup (140g) finely chopped dried figs
1 tablespoon finely chopped fresh chives
8 sheets fillo pastry
cooking-oil spray
1/2 cup (125ml) plum sauce

1 Melt butter in large frying pan; cook onion, cinnamon and garlic, stirring, until onion softens. Add beef; cook, stirring, until browned. Stir in figs and chives; cool 10 minutes.
2 Meanwhile, preheat oven to 200°C/400°F. Oil two oven trays.
3 Coat 1 pastry sheet with oil spray; cover with a second pastry sheet. Cut lengthways into three even strips, then crossways into four strips.
4 Place 1 rounded teaspoon of beef mixture along bottom of one narrow edge of a pastry strip, leaving 1cm (1/2-inch) border. Fold narrow edge over beef mixture then fold in long sides; roll to enclose filling. Place cigar, seam-side down, on trays. Repeat process with remaining pastry and beef mixture.
5 Lightly spray cigars with oil. Bake about 10 minutes or until browned lightly. Serve with plum sauce.

prep + cook time 1 hour **makes** 48
nutritional count per cigar 0.9g total fat (0.4g saturated fat); 142kJ (34 cal); 4.9g carbohydrate; 1.5g protein; 0.6g fibre
tip Keep a plastic spray bottle filled with olive oil in the fridge and bring it to room temperature before using it to spray the fillo. When working with the first two fillo sheets, be sure to cover the remaining sheets with baking paper then a damp tea towel to prevent them drying out.

Meatballs in tomato sauce

2 tablespoons olive oil
1 medium brown onion (150g), chopped finely
3 cloves garlic, crushed
400g (12½ ounces) canned diced tomatoes
meatballs
200g (6½ ounces) minced (ground) beef
200g (6½ ounces) minced (ground) pork
1 small brown onion (80g), chopped finely
½ cup (60g) coarsely grated kasseri cheese
½ cup (35g) stale breadcrumbs
¼ cup finely chopped fresh flat-leaf parsley
1 egg
2 cloves garlic, crushed
1 teaspoon ground cumin

1 Make meatballs.
2 Heat oil in large, non-stick frying pan over medium-high heat; cook meatballs, in batches, until browned. Remove from pan.
3 Cook onion in same pan, stirring, until softened. Stir in garlic; cook until fragrant. Add tomatoes; return meatballs to pan. Bring to the boil; simmer, uncovered, about 10 minutes or until meatballs are cooked through. Season to taste.
meatballs Combine ingredients in medium bowl; season. Roll level tablespoons of mixture into balls.

prep + cook time 35 minutes **makes** 24
nutritional count per meatball 4g total fat (1.4g saturated fat); 264kJ (63 cal); 1.8g carbohydrate; 4.9g protein; 0.6g fibre
tip To shape the meatballs, it's important to chop the onion finely. The secret to round meatballs is to make a circular movement with the pan to roll the meatballs while they cook.
serving suggestion Crusty bread.

Eggplant and haloumi skewers with roasted tomato sauce

1 medium eggplant (300g)
250g (8 ounces) haloumi cheese
¼ cup (35g) plain (all-purpose) flour
1 egg, beaten lightly
½ cup (35g) fresh breadcrumbs
½ cup (40g) finely grated kefalotyri cheese
36 medium fresh basil leaves
vegetable oil, for deep-frying
roasted tomato sauce
125g (4 ounces) cherry tomatoes
cooking-oil spray
1 clove garlic, crushed
1 tablespoon extra virgin olive oil
1 teaspoon red wine vinegar
½ teaspoon white sugar

1 Preheat oven to 180°C/350°F. Make roasted tomato sauce.
2 Meanwhile, cut eggplant and haloumi each into 36 squares.
3 Coat eggplant squares in flour, shake off excess; dip into egg then coat in combined breadcrumbs and kefalotyri.
4 Thread one piece of eggplant, one basil leaf and one piece of haloumi onto each of 36 short bamboo skewers or strong toothpicks. Heat oil in medium saucepan; deep-fry skewers, in batches, 30 seconds or until browned lightly. Drain on absorbent paper.
5 Serve skewers immediately with tomato sauce.
roasted tomato sauce Place tomatoes on baking-paper-lined oven tray; coat with oil spray. Roast 15 minutes or until soft. Blend or process tomatoes with remaining ingredients until smooth. Cool to room temperature.

prep + cook time 55 minutes (+ cooling) **makes** 36
nutritional count per skewer 3.1g total fat (1.2g saturated fat); 192kJ (46 cal); 1.9g carbohydrate; 2.5g protein; 0.4g fibre
tips Soak bamboo skewers in cold water for at least an hour before using to prevent them from scorching during cooking.
Deep-fry these skewers just before serving as the haloumi will toughen on cooling.

Spanakopita

1.5kg (3 pounds) silver beet (swiss chard), trimmed
1 tablespoon olive oil
1 medium brown onion (150g), chopped finely
2 cloves garlic, crushed
1 teaspoon ground nutmeg
200g (6½ ounces) fetta cheese, crumbled
1 tablespoon finely grated lemon rind
¼ cup each coarsely chopped fresh mint, fresh flat-leaf parsley and fresh dill
4 green onions (scallions), chopped finely
16 sheets fillo pastry
125g (4 ounces) butter, melted
2 teaspoons sesame seeds

1 Boil, steam or microwave silver beet until just wilted; drain. When cool enough to handle, squeeze excess liquid from silver beet; drain on absorbent paper. Chop silver beet coarsely; spread out on absorbent paper.
2 Heat oil in small frying pan; cook brown onion and garlic, stirring, until onion is soft. Add nutmeg; cook, stirring, until fragrant. Combine onion mixture and silver beet in large bowl with cheese, rind, herbs and green onion.
3 Preheat oven to 180°C/350°F. Oil oven trays.
4 Brush 1 sheet of pastry with some of the butter; fold lengthways into thirds, brushing with butter between each fold. Place rounded tablespoon of silver beet mixture at one narrow edge of folded pastry sheet, leaving a border. Fold one corner of pastry diagonally over filling to form a large triangle. Continue folding to end of pastry sheet, retaining triangular shape. Repeat with remaining ingredients to make 16 triangles in total.
5 Place triangles, seam-side down, on trays. Brush with remaining butter; sprinkle with sesame seeds. Bake spanakopita about 15 minutes or until browned lightly.

prep + cook time 50 minutes **makes** 16
nutritional count per triangle 11.1g total fat (6.4g saturated fat); 690kJ (165 cal); 11g carbohydrate; 4.7g protein; 1.5g fibre
tips Spanakopita comes from the Greek words spanaki (spinach) and pitta (pie). When working with the first sheet of pastry, cover remaining pastry with a sheet of baking paper then a damp tea towel to prevent it from drying out.

Soups

Lentil soup

1 tablespoon olive oil
1 medium brown onion (150g), chopped finely
2 cloves garlic, crushed
1 cup (200g) brown lentils, rinsed, drained
400g (12½ ounces) canned diced tomatoes
1½ cups (375ml) chicken stock
1½ cups (375ml) water
1 bay leaf
2 tablespoons coarsely chopped fresh dill

1 Heat oil in large saucepan; cook onion, stirring, until softened. Stir in garlic; cook until fragrant.
2 Stir in lentils, undrained tomatoes, stock, the water and bay leaf; bring to the boil. Reduce heat; simmer, covered, about 50 minutes or until lentils are tender. Season to taste. Discard bay leaf.
3 Serve soup sprinkled with dill.

prep + cook time 1 hour **serves** 4
nutritional count per serving 6.2g total fat (1g saturated fat); 880kJ (210 cal); 25.3g carbohydrate; 14.2g protein; 9.2g fibre
serving suggestions A dash of red wine vinegar for each bowl and crusty bread.

Greek chicken and vegetable soup

1.6kg (3¼-pound) whole chicken
1 medium brown onion (150g), halved
1 stalk celery (150g), trimmed, chopped coarsely
3.5 litres (14 cups) water
¼ cup (60ml) olive oil
1 medium brown onion (150g), chopped coarsely
4 medium egg (plum) tomatoes (300g), chopped coarsely
1 large potato (300g), chopped coarsely
2 medium carrots (240g), chopped coarsely
3 stalks celery (450g), trimmed, chopped coarsely, extra
3 bay leaves
1 large zucchini (150g), chopped coarsely
½ cup (110g) soup pasta

1 Rinse chicken under water. Place chicken in large saucepan with halved onion, celery and the water; season. Bring to the boil. Reduce heat; simmer, uncovered, 45 minutes. Skim off any scum as it rises to the surface; discard.
2 Remove chicken from stock; cool 10 minutes. Discard chicken skin and bones; chop chicken flesh coarsely. Strain stock; discard solids.
3 Heat oil in large saucepan; cook chopped onion, stirring, until softened. Add tomato; cook, stirring, 3 minutes. Add potato, carrot, extra celery, bay leaves and strained stock; bring to the boil. Reduce heat; simmer, uncovered, 15 minutes.
4 Return chicken to pan with zucchini and pasta; simmer, uncovered, about 15 minutes or until pasta is tender. Season.

prep + cook time 2 hours (+ cooling) **serves** 8
nutritional count per serving 10.9g total fat (2.3g saturated fat); 1188kJ (284 cal); 18.9g carbohydrate; 27g protein; 4.1g fibre
serving suggestion Crusty bread.

Chicken, lemon and rice soup

2 teaspoons olive oil
1 small brown onion (80g), chopped finely
1 litre (4 cups) chicken stock
400g (12½ ounces) chicken breast fillets, chopped coarsely
⅓ cup (65g) arborio rice
2 eggs
⅓ cup (80ml) lemon juice
2 tablespoons finely chopped fresh flat-leaf parsley

1 Heat oil in large saucepan; cook onion, stirring, until it softens. Add stock, chicken and rice; bring to the boil. Reduce heat; simmer, covered, about 20 minutes or until rice is tender. Remove from heat.
2 Whisk eggs and juice in small bowl until smooth. Gradually whisk ½ cup hot soup into egg mixture, then stir warmed egg mixture back into soup.
3 Serve bowls of soup sprinkled with parsley.

prep + cook time 45 minutes **serves** 4
nutritional count per serving 8.4g total fat (2.3g saturated fat); 1099kJ (263 cal); 16.3g carbohydrate; 30.3g protein; 0.5g fibre
tips This soup is our take on the classic avgolemono (which translates as egg and lemon). There are as many variations of this soup as there are Greek families, but the avgolemono mixture, added near the end of the cooking time, is always the crowning glory.
Arborio rice is an excellent choice for this recipe due to its high starch level, making for a deliciously creamy soup.

Mussel and orzo broth

½ teaspoon saffron threads
½ cup (125ml) ouzo or pernod
4 spring onions (100g)
2 small fennel bulbs (400g)
2 tablespoons olive oil
4 cloves garlic, sliced thinly
2 fresh small red thai (serrano) chillies, sliced thinly
400g (12½ ounces) canned chopped tomatoes
1.5 litres (6 cups) fish stock or water
1 cup (220g) orzo (pasta)
1kg (2 pounds) mussels, cleaned
400g (12½ ounces) firm white fish fillets, chopped coarsely

1 Soak saffron in ouzo in small bowl for 15 minutes.
2 Meanwhile, cut green stems from onions; slice onion stems. Cut onions thinly lengthways. Reserve fennel fronds; slice fennel thinly lengthways. Heat oil in large heavy-based saucepan; cook onion, fennel, garlic and chilli, stirring, about 10 minutes or until onion softens. Add tomato, saffron mixture and stock; bring to the boil.
3 Add orzo; bring to the boil. Reduce heat; simmer, uncovered, stirring occasionally, until orzo is almost tender. Add mussels and fish, return to the boil; simmer, covered, about 5 minutes or until mussels have opened (discard any that do not) and fish is cooked. Season to taste.
4 Stir in chopped fennel fronds and sliced onion stems.

prep + cook time 45 minutes **serves** 6
nutritional count per serving 11.5g total fat (2.4g saturated fat); 1758kJ (420 cal); 41.4g carbohydrate; 27.2g protein; 3.7g fibre
serving suggestion Crusty bread.
tips We used blue-eye in this recipe, but any firm white fish fillet is fine. Orzo is a rice-shaped pasta available from Greek delicatessens and specialty food stores; if unavailable, use risoni.

Lamb and lima bean soup

1 cup (200g) dried lima beans
2 tablespoons olive oil
3 lamb shanks (750g)
2 medium brown onions (300g), chopped finely
1 clove garlic, crushed
2 medium carrots (240g), chopped finely
2 stalks celery (300g), trimmed, chopped finely
2 cups (500ml) chicken stock
1 litre (4 cups) water
400g (12½ ounces) canned chopped tomatoes
¼ cup coarsely chopped fresh dill
2 tablespoons lemon juice

1 Place beans in medium bowl; cover with water. Stand overnight; drain.
2 Heat oil in large saucepan; cook lamb, in batches, until browned all over. Remove from pan.
3 Cook onion, garlic, carrot and celery in same pan, stirring, until onion softens. Return lamb to pan with beans, stock and the water; bring to the boil. Reduce heat; simmer, covered, 1 hour, occasionally skimming off any scum as it rises to the surface.
4 Remove lamb shanks from pan. When cool enough to handle, remove meat from bones. Discard bones; shred meat. Return meat to pan with tomatoes; simmer, covered, 1 hour. Stir in dill and juice.

prep + cook time 2 hours 25 minutes (+ standing) **serves** 8
nutritional count per serving 8.3g total fat (2.1g saturated fat); 928kJ (222 cal); 15.3g carbohydrate; 18.2g protein; 6.8g fibre

Chilled yogurt, cucumber and mint soup

3 medium green cucumbers (510g), peeled, grated coarsely
1 clove garlic, quartered
1 tablespoon lemon juice
1 tablespoon coarsely chopped fresh mint
500g (1 pound) yogurt

1 Place cucumber in sieve over bowl; cover, refrigerate 3 hours or overnight. Reserve cucumber liquid in bowl. Squeeze excess liquid from cucumber.
2 Blend or process cucumber, garlic, juice and mint until smooth; transfer to large bowl. Stir in yogurt; stir in reserved cucumber liquid, a little at a time, until it reaches the desired consistency.

prep time 10 minutes (+ refrigeration) **serves** 4
nutritional count per serving 8.9g total fat (5.7g saturated fat); 715kJ (171 cal); 13.9g carbohydrate; 7.6g protein; 0.8g fibre
serving suggestions Top with fresh mint leaves and toasted bread.

Cream of spinach soup with lemon fetta toasts

40g (1½ ounces) butter
1 large brown onion (200g), chopped finely
2 cloves garlic, crushed
3 medium potatoes (600g), chopped coarsely
3 cups (750ml) chicken stock
4 cups (1 litre) water
1kg (2 pounds) spinach, trimmed, chopped coarsely
¾ cup (180ml) pouring cream
lemon fetta toasts
150g (4½ ounces) fetta cheese
2 teaspoons finely grated lemon rind
1 small french bread stick (150g)

1 Melt butter in large saucepan; cook onion and garlic, stirring, until onion softens. Add potato, stock and the water; bring to the boil. Reduce heat; simmer, covered, about 15 minutes or until potato is tender. Stir in spinach; cool 15 minutes.
2 Meanwhile, make lemon fetta toasts.
3 Blend or process soup, in batches, until smooth. Return soup to same cleaned pan, add cream; stir over medium heat until hot.
4 Serve bowls of soup with toasts.
lemon fetta toasts Preheat grill (broiler). Combine cheese with half the rind. Cut bread into 1.5cm (½-inch) slices; discard end pieces. Toast slices one side; turn, sprinkle each slice with cheese mixture and remaining rind. Grill toasts until browned lightly.

prep + cook time 55 minutes (+ cooling) **serves** 6
nutritional count per serving 19g total fat (12.3g saturated fat); 1078kJ (258 cal); 15.3g carbohydrate; 5.1g protein; 3.6g fibre
nutritional count per toast 6.6g total fat (3.9g saturated fat); 548kJ (131 cal); 11.1g carbohydrate; 6.3g protein; 0.8g fibre

Salads

Capsicum, zucchini and orzo salad

1 medium red capsicum (bell pepper) (200g)
1 medium yellow capsicum (bell pepper) (200g)
1 cup (220g) orzo pasta
2 large zucchini (300g), grated coarsely
½ cup fresh oregano leaves
¼ cup fresh flat-parsley leaves, chopped coarsely
½ cup (75g) seeded kalamata olives, quartered
2 tablespoons olive oil
2 tablespoons red wine vinegar

1 Quarter capsicums; discard seeds and membranes. Roast capsicum, skin-side up, under hot grill or in very hot oven, until skin blisters and blackens. Cover capsicum with plastic or paper for 5 minutes; peel away skin then slice thinly.
2 Meanwhile, cook orzo in large saucepan of boiling salted water until tender; drain.
3 Place capsicum and orzo in large bowl with remaining ingredients; toss gently to combine. Season to taste.

prep + cook time 40 minutes **serves** 4
nutritional count per serving 14.3g total fat (2.1g saturated fat); 1418kJ (339 cal); 43.2g carbohydrate; 8.6g protein; 5.2g fibre
tips Orzo is a rice-shaped pasta available from Greek delicatessens and specialty food stores; if unavailable, use risoni.
To save time, you can buy roasted capsicum pieces from the deli.

Cabbage salad

250g (8 ounces) green cabbage, shredded finely
4 red radishes (60g), sliced thinly
2 tablespoons olive oil
1 ½ tablespoons lemon juice
2 teaspoons finely chopped fresh dill

1 Combine cabbage and radish in large bowl.
2 Just before serving, add combined remaining ingredients to bowl; toss gently to combine. Season to taste.

prep time 10 minutes **serves** 6
nutritional count per serving 6.1g total fat (1g saturated fat); 262kJ (63 cal); 1.3g carbohydrate; 0.7g protein; 1g fibre
tip Use a mandolin or V-slicer if you have one, to finely shred the cabbage.

Eggplant salad

1 large eggplant (500g)
parsley dressing
¼ cup coarsely chopped fresh flat-leaf parsley
1 clove garlic, crushed
1 teaspoon rigani
2 tablespoons olive oil
1 tablespoon lemon juice

1 Preheat oven to 200°C/400°F.
2 Place eggplant on oven tray; prick all over with a fork. Roast eggplant about 40 minutes, turning occasionally, until very soft. Cool; peel.
3 Meanwhile, make parsley dressing.
4 Tear eggplant flesh into long strips. Serve with dressing.
parsley dressing Combine ingredients in small bowl; season to taste.

prep + cook time 50 minutes (+ cooling) **serves** 4 as a side
nutritional count per serving 9.5g total fat (1.5g saturated fat); 424kJ (101 cal); 3.1g carbohydrate; 1.3g protein; 3.1g fibre

Greek salad

¼ cup (60ml) olive oil
1 tablespoon lemon juice
1 tablespoon white wine vinegar
1 tablespoon finely chopped fresh oregano
1 clove garlic, crushed
3 medium tomatoes (450g), cut into wedges
2 lebanese cucumbers (260g), chopped coarsely
200g (6½ ounces) fetta cheese, chopped coarsely
1 small red capsicum (bell pepper) (150g), sliced thinly
1 small red onion (100g), sliced thinly
½ cup (75g) seeded black olives

1 Whisk oil, juice, vinegar, oregano and garlic in large bowl.
2 Add remaining ingredients to bowl; toss gently to combine.

prep time 20 minutes **serves** 4
nutritional count per serving 25.8g total fat (9.6g saturated fat); 1359kJ (325 cal); 10.8g carbohydrate; 11.5g protein; 3.2g fibre

Watermelon and haloumi salad

400g (12½ ounces) watermelon flesh, sliced thinly
180g (5½ ounces) haloumi cheese, sliced thickly
½ cup (80g) kalamata olives, seeded
½ cup loosely packed fresh mint leaves
pickled red onion dressing
1 small red onion (100g), sliced thinly
¼ cup (60ml) red wine vinegar
2 teaspoons caster (superfine) sugar

1 Make pickled red onion dressing.
2 Cut watermelon into wedges, remove rind.
3 Cook cheese, in batches, on heated oiled grill plate (or grill or barbecue or grill pan) until browned. Remove from grill plate.
4 Arrange watermelon and cheese on platter, drizzle with dressing; sprinkle with olives and mint. Season to taste.
pickled red onion dressing Place onion in small heatproof bowl. Stir vinegar and sugar in small saucepan over medium heat until sugar dissolves; bring to the boil. Pour dressing over onion; cool.

prep + cook time 25 minutes (+ cooling) **serves** 4
nutritional count per serving 11.3g total fat (5.5g saturated fat); 795kJ (190 cal); 10.9g carbohydrate; 10.8g protein; 1.8g fibre
tip You will need about 600g (1¼ pounds) watermelon (weighed with skin) for this recipe.

White bean salad

2 x 400g (12½ ounces) canned white beans, rinsed, drained
1 medium red capsicum (bell pepper) (200g), sliced thinly
1 small white onion (80g), sliced thinly
1 cup fresh flat-parsley leaves, shredded finely
½ cup (90g) cornichons, sliced thinly
1 tablespoon rinsed, drained baby capers
2 tablespoons olive oil
¼ cup (60ml) red wine vinegar

1 Place ingredients in medium bowl; toss gently to combine. Season to taste.
2 Stand at room temperature for at least 1 hour before serving.

prep time 15 minutes (+ standing) **serves** 6
nutritional count per serving 6.7g total fat (1.2g saturated fat); 616kJ (147 cal); 16.1g carbohydrate; 6.6g protein; 7.4g fibre
tip Many varieties of cooked white beans are available canned, among them cannellini, butter and haricot beans; any of these are suitable for this recipe.

Pickled zucchini salad

4 medium zucchini (480g)
½ cup fresh dill sprigs
1 tablespoon finely grated lemon rind
pickling liquid
¼ cup (60ml) white wine vinegar
2 teaspoons caster (superfine) sugar
1 teaspoon sea salt
1 tablespoon olive oil

1 Using vegetable peeler, slice zucchini lengthways into ribbons. Combine zucchini, dill and rind in heatproof bowl.
2 Make pickling liquid; pour hot liquid over zucchini mixture. Cool.
pickling liquid Stir vinegar, sugar and salt in small saucepan over medium heat until sugar dissolves; bring to the boil. Remove from heat; stir in oil. Season.

prep + cook time 15 minutes (+ cooling) **serves** 4 as a side
nutritional count per serving 4.9g total fat (0.7g saturated fat); 280kJ (67 cal); 4.2g carbohydrate; 1.1g protein; 1.8g fibre

Spinach, fetta and pine nut salad

50g (1½ ounces) baby spinach leaves
1 cup each loosely packed fresh mint leaves and fresh dill leaves
80g (2½ ounces) soft fetta cheese, crumbled
½ cup (80g) pine nuts, roasted

lemon dressing
1 medium lemon (140g)
1 tablespoon olive oil
1 tablespoon rigani

1 Make lemon dressing.
2 Combine spinach, mint and dill in medium bowl.
3 Just before serving, add cheese, nuts and dressing; toss gently to combine.

lemon dressing Using a zester remove rind from lemon in long thin strips; place in small heatproof bowl. Add enough boiling water to cover rind; drain. Repeat process two more times. Remove remaining skin and pith from lemon. Segment flesh over small bowl to catch juice; coarsely chop flesh. Add well-drained rind and flesh to bowl with juice; add remaining ingredients, season to taste.

prep time 20 minutes **serves** 4
nutritional count per serving 23.3g total fat (4.6g saturated fat); 1040kJ (248 cal); 2g carbohydrate; 7.2g protein; 3.4g fibre

Burghul, tomato and herb salad

1½ cups (240g) burghul (cracked wheat)
300g (9½ ounces) mixed cherry tomatoes, halved
1 cup coarsely chopped fresh flat-leaf parsley
½ cup coarsely chopped fresh mint
6 red radishes (200g), sliced thinly
lemon dressing
⅓ cup (80ml) lemon juice
2 tablespoons olive oil
2 teaspoons finely grated lemon rind

1 Place burghul in medium bowl; pour enough boiling water to cover. Stand burghul about 30 minutes or until tender.
2 Meanwhile, make lemon dressing.
3 Drain burghul in sieve, pressing out as much water as possible; place in large bowl. Add tomatoes, remaining ingredients and dressing; toss gently to combine. Season to taste.
lemon dressing Combine ingredients in small jug.

prep + cook time 15 minutes (+ standing) **serves** 8 as a light meal
nutritional count per serving 5.2g total fat (0.8g saturated fat); 627kJ (150 cal); 20.2g carbohydrate; 3.6g protein; 5.2g fibre.

Roasted vegetable and haloumi salad

¼ cup (60ml) extra virgin olive oil
2 cloves garlic, crushed
1 medium kumara (orange sweet potato) (400g), chopped coarsely
2 large carrots (360g), quartered lengthways
2 medium parsnips (500g), halved lengthways
2 large red onions (600g), cut into wedges
4 baby eggplants (240g), halved lengthways
4 fresh long red chillies, halved
250g (8 ounces) haloumi cheese, sliced
75g (2½ ounces) baby spinach leaves
lemon and basil dressing
½ cup (125ml) extra virgin olive oil
2 tablespoons lemon juice
¼ cup coarsely chopped fresh basil
1 teaspoon white sugar

1 Preheat oven to 220°C/425°F.
2 Combine oil and garlic in small bowl.
3 Combine kumara, carrot and parsnip on large shallow oven tray. Combine onion, eggplant and chilli on another shallow oven tray. Drizzle oil mixture over both trays of vegetables; toss vegetables to coat. Roast kumara mixture about 45 minutes and onion mixture about 30 minutes or until vegetables are cooked and browned lightly.
4 Meanwhile, make lemon and basil dressing.
5 Just before serving, heat oiled grill plate; cook cheese until browned lightly on both sides.
6 Combine roasted vegetables with spinach; divide among serving plates. Top with cheese and drizzle with dressing.
lemon and basil dressing Blend or process ingredients until smooth.

prep + cook time 1 hour **serves** 4
nutritional count per serving 53.6g total fat (12.8g saturated fat); 2880kJ (689 cal); 33g carbohydrate; 20.3g protein; 9.8g fibre
tip Lemon and basil dressing can be made several hours ahead.

Quail, fig and orange salad

6 quails (1.2kg)
3 medium oranges (720g)
4 medium fresh figs (240g), quartered
100g (3 ounces) mizuna
½ cup (60g) coarsely chopped roasted pecans

maple orange dressing
⅓ cup (80ml) orange juice
¼ cup (60ml) olive oil
2 tablespoons pure maple syrup
1 clove garlic, crushed

1 Make maple orange dressing.
2 Rinse quail under cold water; pat dry with absorbent paper. Discard neck from quail. Using kitchen scissors, cut along each side of quail's backbone; discard backbones. Halve quail along breastbone; brush quail halves with half the dressing. Cook quail on heated oiled grill plate (or grill or barbecue) until cooked through.
3 Meanwhile, segment oranges over large bowl. Add remaining ingredients and remaining dressing to bowl; toss gently to combine.
4 Divide salad among serving plates; top with quail.
maple orange dressing Place ingredients in screw-top jar; shake well.

prep + cook time 35 minutes **serves** 4
nutritional count per serving 41.5g total fat (7g saturated fat); 2571kJ (615 cal); 26.8g carbohydrate; 32.3g protein; 5.9g fibre

Lamb and fetta salad with warm walnut dressing

1 tablespoon vegetable oil
600g (1¼ pounds) lamb fillets
250g (8 ounces) witlof (belgian endive), trimmed, leaves separated
200g (6½ ounces) fetta cheese, crumbled
150g (4½ ounces) baby spinach leaves
warm walnut dressing
¼ cup (60ml) olive oil
2 tablespoons cider vinegar
1 teaspoon finely grated lemon rind
2 cloves garlic, crushed
½ cup (55g) coarsely chopped roasted walnuts

1 Heat oil in large frying pan; cook lamb, uncovered, about 10 minutes. Cover; stand 5 minutes then slice thickly.
2 Make warm walnut dressing.
3 Place lamb in medium bowl with witlof, cheese and spinach; toss gently to combine. Serve salad drizzled with dressing.
warm walnut dressing Stir oil, vinegar, rind and garlic in small saucepan over medium heat until hot. Remove from heat; stir in nuts.

prep + cook time 25 minutes **serves** 4
nutritional count per serving 52.8g total fat (16.8g saturated fat); 2742kJ (656 cal); 1.2g carbohydrate; 43.8g protein; 3.2g fibre

Tuna, bean and haloumi salad

500g (1 pound) spinach, trimmed
2 x 420g (13½ ounces) canned four-bean mix, rinsed, drained
425g (13½ ounces) canned tuna in oil, drained, flaked
250g (8 ounces) yellow grape tomatoes, halved
250g (8 ounces) haloumi cheese, cut lengthways into 1cm (½-inch) slices

creamy lemon dressing
½ cup (140g) yogurt
½ teaspoon finely grated lemon rind
¼ cup (60ml) lemon juice
1 teaspoon dijon mustard

1 Boil, steam or microwave spinach until wilted; drain, chop coarsely.
2 Meanwhile, make creamy lemon dressing.
3 Place spinach, beans, tuna and tomato in large bowl; toss gently to combine. Divide salad among serving bowls.
4 Cook cheese in heated oiled large frying pan until browned lightly on both sides.
5 Top salad with cheese; drizzle with dressing.
creamy lemon dressing Place ingredients in screw-top jar; shake well.

prep + cook time 30 minutes **serves** 4
nutritional count per serving 25.8g total fat (10.5g saturated fat); 2278kJ (545 cal); 25.6g carbohydrate; 47.1g protein; 11.4g fibre
serving suggestion Lemon wedges.

Peppered lamb with watercress, pea and mint salad

2 tablespoons mixed peppercorns
1 tablespoon olive oil
600g (1¼ pounds) lamb fillets
1 cup (160g) fresh or frozen peas
250g (8 ounces) yellow teardrop tomatoes, halved
100g (3 ounces) watercress, trimmed
200g (6½ ounces) fetta cheese, cut into thin strips
¼ cup coarsely chopped fresh mint

white wine vinaigrette
¼ cup (60ml) white wine vinegar
1 tablespoon olive oil
1 clove garlic, crushed

1 Using mortar and pestle, crush peppercorns until coarsely ground. Combine ground peppercorns, oil and lamb in medium bowl.
2 Cook lamb in heated oiled large frying pan until cooked as desired. Cover lamb; stand 5 minutes then slice thinly.
3 Meanwhile, make white wine vinaigrette.
4 Boil, steam or microwave peas until tender; drain. Rinse under cold water; drain.
5 Place lamb and peas in large bowl with vinaigrette and remaining ingredients; toss gently to combine.
white wine vinaigrette Place ingredients in screw-top jar; shake well.

prep + cook time 30 minutes **serves** 4
nutritional count per serving 31.1g total fat (12g saturated fat); 2006kJ (480 cal); 5.1g carbohydrate; 43.2g protein; 5g fibre

Wild rice salad with lemon and garlic yogurt

2 cups (400g) wild rice blend
1 medium red capsicum (bell pepper) (200g)
1 medium brown onion (150g), quartered
250g (8 ounces) cherry tomatoes
350g (11 ounces) broccolini, halved crossways
½ cup (80g) roasted pine nuts
1 cup coarsely chopped fresh flat-leaf parsley
2 tablespoons lemon juice
lemon and garlic yogurt
2 cloves garlic, crushed
1 cup (280g) yogurt
¼ cup (60ml) lemon juice

1 Cook rice in large saucepan of boiling water, uncovered, until tender; drain. Place in large serving bowl.
2 Make lemon and garlic yogurt.
3 Quarter capsicum; discard seeds and membranes. Cook capsicum, onion and tomatoes on heated, oiled grill plate (or grill or barbecue) until tender. Chop capsicum and onion coarsely.
4 Boil, steam or microwave broccolini until tender.
5 Combine capsicum, onion, tomatoes, nuts, parsley and juice with rice. Serve salad topped with broccolini then yogurt.
lemon and garlic yogurt Combine ingredients in small bowl.

prep + cook time 35 minutes **serves** 6
nutritional count per serving 11.6g total fat (1.7g saturated fat); 1007kJ (241 cal); 20.2g carbohydrate; 10.9g protein; 6.3g fibre
tip Wild rice blend is a pre-made mixture of white long-grain and wild rice. The latter, the seed of a North American aquatic grass, has a distinctively nutty flavour and crunchy, resilient texture.

Beetroot, pumpkin and spinach salad with fetta polenta

2 cups (500ml) water
2 cups (500ml) vegetable stock
1 cup (170g) polenta
200g (6½ ounces) fetta cheese, crumbled
10 small beetroots (beets) (600g)
2 tablespoons olive oil
700g (1½ pounds) peeled pumpkin, cut into 4cm (1½-inch) pieces
150g (4½ ounces) baby spinach leaves
¾ cup (75g) roasted walnuts, chopped coarsely
walnut vinaigrette
2 tablespoons walnut oil
¼ cup (60ml) olive oil
¼ cup (60ml) lemon juice

1 Preheat oven to 200°C/400°F. Oil 20cm x 30cm (8-inch x 12-inch) lamington pan; line with baking paper.
2 Bring the water and stock to the boil in large saucepan. Gradually add polenta, stirring constantly. Reduce heat; cook, stirring, about 10 minutes or until polenta thickens. Stir in cheese. Spread polenta into pan; cool 10 minutes. Cover; refrigerate about 1 hour or until polenta is firm.
3 Meanwhile, discard beetroot stems and leaves; quarter unpeeled beetroots. Place in large shallow baking dish, drizzle with half the oil; roast, uncovered, 15 minutes. Add pumpkin, drizzle with remaining oil; roast, uncovered, about 30 minutes or until vegetables are tender.
4 Make walnut vinaigrette.
5 When cool enough to handle, peel beetroot. Place in large bowl with dressing; toss gently to combine.
6 Turn polenta onto board; trim edges. Cut polenta into 12 pieces; cook, in batches, on heated oiled grill plate (or grill or barbecue) until browned both sides and heated through.
7 Add pumpkin, spinach and nuts to beetroot mixture; toss gently to combine. Divide polenta pieces among serving plates; top with salad.
walnut vinaigrette Place ingredients in screw-top jar; shake well.

prep + cook time 1 hour 35 minutes (+ refrigeration) **serves** 4
nutritional count per serving 58.8g total fat (13.3g saturated fat); 3403kJ (814 cal); 51.8g carbohydrate; 23g protein; 9.3g fibre

Beetroot, asparagus and fetta salad

340g (11 ounces) asparagus, halved crossways
200g (6½ ounces) fetta cheese, crumbled
1 cup loosely packed fresh mint leaves, torn
450g (14½ ounces) canned beetroot (beets) wedges, drained
½ cup (50g) roasted walnut halves
lemon dressing
¼ cup (60ml) olive oil
1 ½ tablespoons lemon juice
1 clove garlic, crushed

1 Make lemon dressing.
2 Boil, steam or microwave asparagus until just tender; drain.
3 Place asparagus and dressing in large bowl with remaining ingredients; toss gently to combine.
lemon dressing Place ingredients in screw-top jar; shake well.

prep + cook time 15 minutes **serves** 6
nutritional count per serving 22.8g total fat (6.8g saturated fat); 1129kJ (270 cal); 6.2g carbohydrate; 9.1g protein; 3.1g fibre
tip To ensure walnuts roast evenly, place ¾ cup unroasted nuts in a small microwave-safe bowl; microwave on HIGH about 2 minutes, pausing and stirring every 30 seconds, until the nuts are fragrant and slightly browner in colour. Spread walnuts on absorbent paper until cool. This method also works well for almonds, pine nuts, hazelnuts and cashews.

Green salad with fennel and herbs

1 baby cos lettuce (180g), shredded finely
200g (6½ ounces) rocket (arugula), trimmed
100g (3 ounces) watercress, trimmed
5 green onions (scallions), chopped finely
1 small fennel (200g), sliced thinly
¼ cup coarsely chopped fresh dill
½ cup loosely packed fresh mint leaves
½ cup (80g) roasted pine nuts
red wine vinaigrette
¼ cup (60ml) olive oil
¼ cup (60ml) red wine vinegar

1 Make red wine vinaigrette.
2 Place lettuce, rocket, watercress, onion, fennel and herbs in large bowl with vinaigrette and nuts; toss gently to combine.
red wine vinaigrette Place ingredients in screw-top jar; shake well.

prep time 15 minutes **serves** 8
nutritional count per serving 14.2g total fat (1.4g saturated fat); 635kJ (152 cal); 2.4g carbohydrate; 3g protein; 2.6g fibre

Prawn, pink grapefruit and fetta salad

24 cooked large king prawns (shrimp) (1.6kg)
1 baby cos lettuce (180g), trimmed, leaves separated
2 small pink grapefruits (700g), segmented
200g (6½ ounces) fetta cheese, crumbled

chilli mint dressing

¼ cup (60ml) olive oil
¼ cup (60ml) red wine vinegar
1 teaspoon sugar
¼ cup coarsely chopped fresh mint
1 fresh long red chilli, sliced thinly

1 Shell and devein prawns, leaving tails intact.

2 Make chilli mint dressing.

3 Divide lettuce, prawns, grapefruit and cheese among serving plates; drizzle with dressing.

chilli mint dressing Place ingredients in screw-top jar; shake well.

prep time 30 minutes **serves** 8

nutritional count per serving 17.9g total fat (6.5g saturated fat); 1346kJ (322 cal); 5.1g carbohydrate; 34.5g protein; 1.2g fibre

Mains

CHICKEN + RABBIT

Roasted garlic, lemon and oregano chicken

1.5kg (3 pounds) medium potatoes, quartered lengthways
4 chicken marylands (1.4kg)
½ cup (125ml) lemon juice
½ cup (125ml) olive oil
6 cloves garlic, chopped finely
2 teaspoons rigani
1½ cups (375ml) water

1 Preheat oven to 180°C/350°F.
2 Place potatoes in large baking dish; top with chicken. Combine juice, oil, garlic and rigani in small jug; pour over chicken and potatoes, then add the water. Season with salt and ground white pepper.
3 Roast chicken and potatoes about 1½ hours or until chicken is tender and browned.

prep + cook time 1 hour 40 minutes **serves** 4
nutritional count per serving 46.2g total fat (9.8g saturated fat); 3793kJ (906 cal); 48.1g carbohydrate; 73.5g protein; 7.3g fibre
serving suggestion Green salad.

Chicken pilaf

2 tablespoons olive oil
1.5kg (3 pounds) chicken pieces
1 large brown onion (200g), sliced thinly
4 cloves garlic, sliced thinly
2 teaspoons rigani
1 tablespoon fresh thyme leaves
800g (1½ pounds) canned whole tomatoes
1½ cups (375ml) chicken stock
1½ cups (300g) white long-grain rice
¼ cup coarsely chopped fresh flat-leaf parsley

1 Heat oil in large saucepan; cook chicken, in batches, until browned. Remove from pan.
2 Cook onion and garlic in same pan, stirring, until onion softens. Add rigani, thyme, undrained tomatoes and stock; bring to the boil. Return chicken to pan; season with salt and pepper. Cook, covered, over low heat, about 1 hour.
3 Remove chicken from pan; cover to keep warm. Stir rice into pan; cook, covered tightly, over low heat, without stirring, 15 minutes. Remove from heat; stand, covered, 5 minutes. Stir in half the parsley. Season to taste.
4 Divide rice mixture among serving plates; top with chicken and remaining parsley.

prep + cook time 1 hour 35 minutes **serves** 4
nutritional count per serving 35.2g total fat (9.3g saturated fat); 3407kJ (814 cal); 68g carbohydrate; 55.6g protein; 4.8g fibre

Lemon and dill chicken

2 tablespoons olive oil
30g (1 ounce) butter
1.5kg (3 pounds) chicken thigh cutlets (skin on)
2 medium brown onions (300g), sliced thinly
1 large carrot (180g), sliced thickly
1 stalk celery (150g), trimmed, sliced thickly
2 tablespoons plain (all-purpose) flour
2 cups (500ml) water
2 tablespoons finely chopped fresh dill
3 egg yolks
⅓ cup (80ml) lemon juice

1 Heat oil and butter in large saucepan; cook chicken, in batches, over medium heat until sealed on both sides but not coloured. Remove from pan.
2 Cook onion, carrot, celery and flour in same pan, stirring, 1 minute. Gradually add the water; bring to the boil. Return chicken to pan. Reduce heat; simmer, covered, 30 minutes. Remove lid; simmer, uncovered, about 30 minutes or until chicken is cooked through. Season to taste; sprinkle with dill.
3 Whisk egg yolks and juice together in small bowl. Gradually add to chicken mixture, stirring over low heat, until sauce thickens slightly.

prep + cook time 1 hour 25 minutes **serves** 6
nutritional count per serving 43.6g total fat (13.9g saturated fat); 2224kJ (530 cal); 7.1g carbohydrate; 29g protein; 2.4g fibre
tip Egg whites can be placed in a small container, sealed, and frozen for up to 3 months. They can be used in meringue, pavlova and friands.
serving suggestions Steamed long-grain rice and green salad.

Rabbit stifado

1.4kg (2¾-pound) whole rabbit
⅔ cup (160ml) dry red wine
⅓ cup (80ml) red wine vinegar
2 cloves garlic, crushed
3 bay leaves
1 cinnamon stick
6 cloves
1 tablespoon light brown sugar
2 teaspoons rigani
½ teaspoon ground allspice
¼ cup (60ml) olive oil
800g (1½ pounds) baby brown onions, peeled
2 tablespoons tomato paste
1 litre (4 cups) water
2 tablespoons coarsely chopped fresh flat-leaf parsley

1 Chop rabbit into eight even-sized pieces. Combine rabbit, wine, vinegar, garlic, bay leaves, cinnamon, cloves, sugar, rigani and allspice in large bowl. Cover; refrigerate 3 hours or overnight.
2 Heat oil in large saucepan; cook onions, stirring, over medium heat, until softened. Remove from pan.
3 Remove rabbit from marinade; reserve marinade. Cook rabbit in same heated pan, in batches, until browned. Remove from pan.
4 Return rabbit and onions to pan with paste, the water and reserved marinade; bring to the boil. Reduce heat; simmer, uncovered, over low heat, about 2 hours or until sauce has thickened. Season. Serve topped with parsley.

prep + cook time 2 hours 35 minutes (+ refrigeration) **serves** 4
nutritional count per serving 27.9g total fat (5.7g saturated fat); 2284kJ (546 cal); 12.8g carbohydrate; 54.3g protein; 4.6g fibre
tip Ask the butcher to chop the rabbit into pieces for you.
serving suggestion Crusty bread.

Rabbit with olives, parsley and pine nuts

1.4kg (2¾-pound) whole rabbit
1 cup (150g) fetta-stuffed green olives
½ cup loosely packed fresh flat-leaf parsley leaves
⅓ cup (50g) pine nuts, roasted
1½ cups (375ml) dry white wine
½ cup (125ml) water
½ cup (125ml) olive oil
2 teaspoons finely chopped fresh rosemary

1 Preheat oven to 160°C/325°F. Oil large baking dish.
2 Rinse rabbit under cold water; pat dry inside and out with absorbent paper. Place rabbit in baking dish; fill cavity of rabbit with combined olives, parsley and pine nuts. Tie at intervals with kitchen string.
3 Combine wine, the water, oil and rosemary in small jug; pour over rabbit. Season with salt and pepper.
4 Roast rabbit about 1½ hours or until rabbit is tender. Serve rabbit drizzled with pan juices.

prep + cook time 1 hour 45 minutes **serves** 4
nutritional count per serving 54.3g total fat (9g saturated fat); 3098kJ (740 cal); 2.4g carbohydrate; 53g protein; 2.1g fibre
serving suggestions Crusty bread and green salad.

Spicy reddened chicken with pasta

2 tablespoons olive oil
1.5kg (3 pounds) chicken pieces
1 large brown onion (200g), chopped finely
6 cloves garlic, crushed
⅓ cup (90g) tomato paste
1 tablespoon finely chopped fresh basil
2 teaspoons cayenne pepper
½ teaspoon each ground clove, nutmeg and cinnamon
2 tablespoons brandy
400g (12½ ounces) canned tomato puree
2 cups (500ml) water
375g (12 ounces) penne rigate
1 cup (80g) finely grated kefalotyri cheese

1 Heat oil in large saucepan; cook chicken, in batches, until browned. Remove from pan.
2 Cook onion and garlic in same pan, stirring, until onion softens. Add paste, basil, spices and brandy; cook, stirring, 1 minute. Return chicken to pan with puree and the water; bring to the boil. Reduce heat; simmer, covered, about 50 minutes or until chicken is cooked through.
3 Remove chicken from pan; discard skin and bones; chop chicken flesh coarsely.
4 Meanwhile, cook pasta in large saucepan of boiling salted water until tender; drain.
5 Combine chicken and pasta with tomato mixture; season to taste. Sprinkle with cheese.

prep + cook time 1 hour 20 minutes **serves** 4
nutritional count per serving 27g total fat (8.4g saturated fat); 3365kJ (804 cal); 77g carbohydrate; 56.9g protein; 7.2g fibre
tip You could use pecorino cheese as a substitute for kefalotyri cheese.

Chicken and okra stew

2 tablespoons olive oil
1.5kg (3 pounds) chicken drumsticks
1 large brown onion (200g), chopped finely
3 cloves garlic, crushed
2 tablespoons tomato paste
1 teaspoon cayenne pepper
400g (12½ ounces) canned tomato puree
1 cup (250ml) chicken stock
1 cup (250ml) water
200g (6½ ounces) okra

1 Heat oil in large saucepan; cook chicken, in batches, until browned. Remove from pan.
2 Cook onion and garlic in same pan, stirring, until onion softens. Add paste and pepper; cook, stirring, 1 minute. Return chicken to pan with tomato puree, stock and the water; bring to the boil. Reduce heat; simmer, covered, 40 minutes.
3 Add okra; simmer, uncovered, about 15 minutes or until chicken is cooked through and okra is tender. Season to taste.

prep + cook time 1 hour 15 minutes **serves** 4
nutritional count per serving 32.7g total fat (8.5g saturated fat); 2205kJ (527 cal); 11g carbohydrate; 47.3g protein; 4.3g fibre
serving suggestion Steamed long-grain rice.

Chicken fillo pie

500g (1 pound) chicken breast fillets, halved
500g (1 pound) chicken thigh fillets, halved
3 cups (750ml) salt-reduced chicken stock
80g (2½ ounces) butter, chopped
1 small brown onion (80g), chopped finely
⅓ cup (50g) plain (all-purpose) flour
200g (6½ ounces) fetta cheese, crumbled
¼ cup each of finely chopped fresh flat-leaf parsley, dill and mint
1 teaspoon ground nutmeg
4 eggs, beaten lightly
8 sheets fillo pastry
¼ cup (60ml) olive oil

1 Place chicken and stock in medium saucepan; bring to simmer. Simmer, uncovered, 15 minutes. Remove from heat; cover, stand 15 minutes. Remove chicken from stock. Chop chicken coarsely; strain, reserve 2 cups of the stock. Keep remaining stock for another use.
2 Melt butter in medium saucepan; cook onion, stirring, until onion softens. Add flour; cook, stirring, 1 minute. Gradually stir in hot reserved stock; cook, stirring, over medium heat until mixture boils and thickens. Remove from heat; cool 15 minutes.
3 Preheat oven to 180°C/350°F. Oil 24cm (9½-inch) springform tin.
4 Place chicken and sauce mixture in large bowl, combine with cheese, herbs, nutmeg and egg; season.
5 Brush 1 sheet of pastry with oil; top with remaining sheets, brushing each with oil. Line tin with pastry; pour in chicken filling. Roll edges of pastry and tuck down side of tin.
6 Bake pie about 1¼ hours or until browned and set. Stand pie in tin 15 minutes before serving.

prep + cook time 2 hours 10 minutes (+ standing & cooling) **serves** 8
nutritional count per serving 29.9g total fat (12.9g saturated fat); 1955kJ (467 cal); 14.5g carbohydrate; 35.1g protein; 1.1g fibre
tip Remaining chicken stock can be used in soups, sauces and casseroles. If not using within 3 days, freeze.
serving suggestions Serve warm or cold with green salad.

Braised chickens with fennel and ouzo

¼ cup (60ml) olive oil
4 small chickens (poussin) (2kg)
1 medium lemon (140g), quartered
2 large fennel bulbs (1kg), halved, sliced thinly
1 large brown onion (200g), sliced thinly
2 cloves garlic, sliced thinly
¼ cup (60ml) ouzo
2 cups (500ml) chicken stock
3 large zucchini (450g), sliced thinly
2 tablespoons lemon juice
½ cup (125ml) pouring cream
2 tablespoons coarsely chopped fennel fronds

1 Preheat oven to 200°C/400°F.
2 Heat 1 tablespoon of the oil in large deep flameproof baking dish; cook chickens, one at a time, until browned all over. Remove from dish. Place one lemon quarter in cavity of each chicken.
3 Heat remaining oil in same dish; cook fennel, onion and garlic, stirring, until onion softens. Add ouzo; cook, stirring, until ouzo evaporates. Add stock; bring to the boil. Place chickens on fennel mixture; roast about 35 minutes or until chickens are just cooked through.
4 Add zucchini to dish, submerging into fennel mixture; roast, uncovered, about 5 minutes or until zucchini is tender. Transfer chickens to large plate; cover to keep warm.
5 Bring fennel mixture to the boil. Add juice and cream; return to the boil. Reduce heat; simmer, uncovered, 5 minutes. Stir in half the fennel fronds.
6 Using slotted spoon, divide fennel mixture among plates; top with chicken. Drizzle with pan juices; sprinkle with remaining fennel fronds.

prep + cook time 1 hour 40 minutes **serves** 4
nutritional count per serving 61.4g total fat (20.8g saturated fat); 3407kJ (815 cal); 10g carbohydrate; 49.1g protein; 6.4g fibre
serving suggestions Orzo or risoni.

Roast chickens with dill and walnut pesto

⅓ cup firmly packed fresh flat-leaf parsley leaves
½ cup firmly packed fresh dill sprigs
½ cup (50g) roasted walnuts, chopped coarsely
¼ cup (20g) finely grated kefalotyri cheese
¼ cup (60ml) lemon juice
¼ cup (60ml) olive oil
4 small chickens (poussin) (2kg)
2 medium lemons (280g), quartered

risoni salad
1 cup (220g) risoni
6 slices pancetta (90g), chopped finely
⅓ cup (50g) roasted pine nuts
¼ cup each finely chopped fresh basil and flat-leaf parsley
2 tablespoons olive oil
1 tablespoon red wine vinegar

1 Preheat oven to 180°C/350°F.
2 Blend or process herbs, nuts, cheese and juice until combined. With motor operating, gradually add oil in thin, steady stream until pesto thickens slightly. Reserve 1 tablespoon of pesto for risoni salad.
3 Wash chickens under cold water. Discard necks; pat dry inside and out with absorbent paper. Loosen chicken skin; rub remaining pesto between skin and flesh and over outside of chickens. Place 2 lemon quarters in cavity of each chicken.
4 Place chickens on oiled wire rack over baking dish; roast, uncovered, about 45 minutes or until cooked through.
5 Meanwhile, make risoni salad.
6 Remove chickens from baking dish; discard pan juices. Halve chickens lengthways; serve chickens with salad.
risoni salad Cook pasta in large saucepan of boiling water until just tender; drain. Cook pancetta in small heated non-stick frying pan, stirring, about 5 minutes or until crisp. Place pasta and pancetta in large bowl with remaining ingredients and reserved pesto; toss gently to combine.

prep + cook time 1 hour 40 minutes **serves** 4
nutritional count per serving 85.1g total fat (18.9g saturated fat); 5029kJ (1203 cal); 40.3g carbohydrate; 65.5g protein; 5.5g fibre

Chicken drumsticks with olives and artichokes

2 tablespoons olive oil
12 chicken drumsticks (1.8kg)
1 medium white onion (150g), chopped finely
3 cloves garlic, crushed
1 tablespoon finely grated lemon rind
1½ cups (375ml) chicken stock
½ cup (125ml) dry white wine
340g (11 ounces) bottled marinated artichokes, drained, quartered
500g (1 pound) risoni
2 tablespoons finely chopped fresh oregano
1 cup (150g) seeded black olives
1 tablespoon finely grated lemon rind, extra
¼ cup (60ml) lemon juice

1 Heat half the oil in large heavy-based saucepan; cook drumsticks, in batches, until browned all over. Remove from pan.
2 Heat remaining oil in same pan; cook onion and garlic, stirring, until onion softens. Add rind, stock, wine and artichokes; bring to the boil. Return drumsticks to pan, reduce heat; simmer, covered, 20 minutes. Uncover; simmer, 10 minutes or until drumsticks are cooked through.
3 Meanwhile, cook risoni in large saucepan of boiling water until just tender; drain.
4 Remove chicken from pan; stir oregano, olives, extra juice and extra rind into sauce.
5 Serve chicken and sauce on risoni.

prep + cook time 1 hour 15 minutes **serves** 4
nutritional count per serving 44.7g total fat (11.7g saturated fat); 4631kJ (1108 cal); 98.7g carbohydrate; 67.8g protein; 5.7g fibre

Chicken, tomato and fetta patties with spinach salad

750g (1½ pounds) minced (ground) chicken
⅓ cup (50g) drained semi-dried tomatoes, chopped coarsely
1 egg
½ cup (35g) fresh breadcrumbs
200g (6½ ounces) fetta cheese, crumbled
1 small white onion (80g), sliced thinly
100g (3 ounces) baby spinach leaves
1 tablespoon olive oil
1 tablespoon balsamic vinegar

1 Combine chicken, tomato, egg, breadcrumbs and half the cheese in large bowl; shape mixture into 12 patties.
2 Cook patties in heated oiled large frying pan, in batches, until cooked through. Drain on absorbent paper.
3 Meanwhile, combine onion, spinach, oil, vinegar and remaining cheese in medium bowl.
4 Serve patties with spinach salad.

prep + cook time 30 minutes **serves** 4
nutritional count per serving 33.7g total fat (13.3g saturated fat); 2320kJ (555 cal); 11.8g carbohydrate; 50.1g protein; 3.2g fibre

Chicken and haloumi skewers with pilaf

2½ cups (625ml) chicken stock
25g (¾ ounce) butter
1 medium brown onion (150g), chopped finely
1⅓ cups (265g) basmati rice, rinsed, drained
1 bay leaf
600g (1¼ pounds) chicken breast fillets, cut into 2cm (¾-inch) pieces
250g (8 ounces) haloumi cheese, cut into 16 pieces
8 cherry tomatoes
2 tablespoons olive oil

lemon yogurt sauce
1 cup (280g) yogurt
2 tablespoons finely chopped fresh flat-leaf parsley
1 teaspoon finely grated lemon rind
1 tablespoon lemon juice
½ clove garlic, crushed

1 Heat stock in small saucepan.
2 Melt butter in large saucepan; cook onion, stirring, until soft. Add rice and bay leaf; cook, stirring, 2 minutes. Add stock; simmer, covered, about 10 minutes or until rice is tender and liquid is absorbed.
3 Meanwhile, make lemon yogurt sauce.
4 Thread chicken, cheese and tomatoes alternately onto skewers; brush with oil. Cook skewers on heated oiled grill plate (or grill or barbecue) until chicken is cooked.
5 Serve skewers with pilaf and lemon yogurt sauce.
lemon yogurt sauce Combine ingredients in small bowl.

prep + cook time 45 minutes **serves** 4
nutritional count per serving 39.1g total fat (17.7g saturated fat); 3494kJ (836 cal); 63.9g carbohydrate; 56.2g protein; 1.8g fibre
tip Soak bamboo skewers in water for 1 hour before using to prevent them scorching during cooking.

Barbecued chicken with minted tomato salad

2 tablespoons lemon juice
1 tablespoon sumac
2 teaspoons finely chopped fresh oregano
2 tablespoons olive oil
6 x 200g (6½-ounce) chicken breast fillets
3 medium lemons (420g), halved
3 large pitta bread (240g)

minted tomato salad
2 tablespoons lemon juice
2 tablespoons olive oil
500g (1 pound) grape tomatoes, halved
2 lebanese cucumbers (260g), cut into ribbons
1 cup each firmly packed fresh flat-leaf parsley leaves and fresh mint leaves
2 teaspoons finely chopped fresh oregano
8 green onions (scallions), sliced thinly

1 Combine juice, sumac, oregano and half the oil in large bowl with chicken. Cover; refrigerate 3 hours or overnight.
2 Make minted tomato salad.
3 Cook chicken on barbecue (or grill or grill plate) until browned both sides and cooked through. Stand 5 minutes then slice thickly.
4 Cook lemon, cut-side down, about 3 minutes or until browned lightly. Brush bread, both sides, with remaining oil; brown lightly on barbecue, break into coarse pieces.
5 Combine salad and bread; serve with chicken and lemon.
minted tomato salad Whisk juice and oil in large serving bowl, add remaining ingredients; toss gently to combine.

prep + cook time 35 minutes (+ refrigeration) **serves** 6
nutritional count per serving 24.4g total fat (5.2g saturated fat); 2199kJ (526 cal); 25.6g carbohydrate; 48.2g protein; 5.4g fibre
tips Refrigerate the chicken overnight, if you can, for the best flavour. Salad ingredients can be prepared ahead; assemble just before serving.

Barbecued lemon thyme chicken

6 cloves garlic, sliced thickly
3 shallots (75g), chopped finely
½ cup (125ml) chicken stock
20g (¾ ounce) butter, softened
1 tablespoon finely chopped fresh lemon thyme
1.6kg (3¼-pound) whole chicken
600g (1¼ pounds) kipfler potatoes, halved lengthways
340g (11 ounces) asparagus, trimmed
1 medium lemon (140g), quartered
1 tablespoon olive oil

1 Place garlic, shallot and stock in small saucepan; bring to the boil. Reduce heat; simmer, uncovered, about 20 minutes or until garlic is soft and liquid is almost evaporated. Cool 5 minutes; stir in butter and thyme.
2 Wash chicken under cold water; pat dry inside and out with absorbent paper. Using kitchen scissors, cut along each side of backbone; discard backbone. Place chicken, skin-side up, on board. Using heel of hand, press down on breastbone to flatten chicken. Make a pocket between chicken and skin; push thyme mixture under skin.
3 Cook chicken, skin-side down, on heated oiled grill plate (or grill or barbecue), covered, over medium heat, 15 minutes. Turn chicken; cook, covered, about 35 minutes or until cooked through. Cover; stand 15 minutes.
4 Meanwhile, boil, steam or microwave potato until just tender; drain. Cook potato, asparagus and lemon on same grill plate (or grill or barbecue) brushing with oil, until browned.
5 Serve chicken with potato, asparagus and lemon.

prep + cook time 1 hour 45 minutes (+ standing) **serves** 4
nutritional count per serving 41.4g total fat (13.5g saturated fat); 2776kJ (664 cal); 22.8g carbohydrate; 46.7g protein; 5.4g fibre

Oregano chicken with greek salad

750g (1 ½ pounds) chicken breast fillets
2 tablespoons lemon juice
2 tablespoons olive oil
1 tablespoon finely chopped fresh oregano
1 clove garlic, crushed
1 baby cos lettuce (180g), trimmed, chopped coarsely
3 medium tomatoes (450g), cut into wedges
1 lebanese cucumber (130g), chopped coarsely
½ small red onion (40g), sliced thinly
½ cup (75g) seeded kalamata olives
125g (4 ounces) fetta cheese, crumbled coarsely
dressing
¼ cup (60ml) olive oil
2 tablespoons red wine vinegar
2 tablespoons lemon juice
½ teaspoon rigani
½ teaspoon caster (superfine) sugar

1 Combine chicken, juice, oil, oregano and garlic in medium bowl; season. Cover; refrigerate 30 minutes.
2 Meanwhile, make dressing.
3 Cook chicken on heated oiled grill plate (or grill or barbecue or grill pan) until cooked through. Slice chicken thickly.
4 Combine lettuce, tomato, cucumber, onion, olives and fetta in large bowl. Divide salad among plates; top with chicken, drizzle with dressing.
dressing Place ingredients in screw-top jar; shake well. Season.

prep + cook time 30 minutes (+ refrigeration) **serves** 4
nutritional count per serving 37g total fat (9.8g saturated fat); 2347kJ (560 cal); 6.5g carbohydrate; 49.9g protein; 3.4g fibre

Grilled lemon chicken

½ cup (125ml) olive oil
½ cup (125ml) lemon juice
1.5kg (3 pounds) chicken thigh fillets
2 teaspoons rigani
2 teaspoons coarse cooking salt
1 teaspoon ground white pepper
1 medium lemon (140g), cut into wedges

1 Blend or process oil and juice until thick and creamy.
2 Combine chicken, rigani, salt, pepper and half the lemon mixture in medium bowl. Thread chicken onto eight oiled metal skewers.
3 Cook skewers on heated oiled grill plate (or grill or barbecue or grill pan), brushing frequently with remaining lemon mixture until cooked through.
4 Serve skewers with lemon wedges.

prep + cook time 30 minutes **serves** 8
nutritional count per serving 30g total fat (7g saturated fat); 1690kJ (404 cal); 1g carbohydrate; 33g protein; 0.1g fibre
serving suggestion Green salad.

SEAFOOD

Barbecued vine-leaf-wrapped sardines

12 small whole sardines (500g), cleaned
1 medium lemon (140g), halved, sliced thinly
12 fresh bay leaves
12 small preserved vine leaves
1 tablespoon olive oil
garlic and lemon potatoes
2 tablespoons olive oil
600g (1¼ pounds) small potatoes, sliced thinly
1 medium lemon (140g)
4 cloves garlic, sliced thinly

1 Rinse cavities of sardines, pat dry. Season cavities; top each sardine with a lemon slice and a bay leaf. Wrap each sardine tightly in a vine leaf to enclose lemon and bay leaf, leaving heads and tails exposed. Brush sardines with oil.
2 Make garlic and lemon potatoes.
3 Meanwhile, cook sardines on heated oiled grill plate (or grill or barbecue or grill pan), until cooked through.
4 Serve sardines with potatoes and lemon wedges.
garlic and lemon potatoes Heat oil in large frying pan; cook potatoes, turning, about 15 minutes until starting to soften and brown. Remove rind from whole lemon using a zester, add to potatoes with garlic; cook, stirring, until potatoes and garlic are cooked through. Season to taste.

prep + cook time 1 hour **serves** 4
nutritional count per serving 20g total fat (3.9g saturated fat); 1686kJ (403 cal); 17g carbohydrate; 37.9g protein; 3.6g fibre
tip Preserved vine leaves are available in cryovac packets from some delicatessens and Middle Eastern food shops; they must be rinsed well and dried before using.
serving suggestion Sliced tomato and white onion salad.

Squid stuffed with rice, currants and pine nuts

12 small squid (800g)
¼ cup (60ml) olive oil
1 medium onion (150g), chopped finely
2 cloves garlic, chopped finely
½ cup (100g) white long-grain rice
¾ cup (180ml) fish stock
2 tablespoons dried currants
2 tablespoons roasted pine nuts
25g (¾ ounce) baby spinach leaves, sliced thinly
1 tablespoon finely shredded fresh mint leaves
1 teaspoon finely grated lemon rind
2 tablespoons lemon juice

1 Clean squid; reserve tentacles and wing. Cut tentacles and wings into small pieces.
2 Heat 1 tablespoon of the oil in medium heavy-based saucepan; cook onion and garlic, stirring, until onion softens. Add rice; stir to coat in onion mixture. Stir in squid pieces, stock, currants and pine nuts. Simmer, covered tightly, about 10 minutes or until liquid has evaporated and rice is tender.
3 Stir spinach, mint, rind and juice into rice mixture; season. Spoon rounded tablespoons mixture into squid tubes leaving 1cm (½-inch) gap; secure ends with toothpicks.
4 Preheat oven to 180°C/350°F.
5 Heat remaining oil in large frying pan; cook squid, in batches, until browned lightly. Transfer squid to oven tray, roast uncovered, about 5 minutes or until squid is opaque and filling is heated through.

prep + cook time 1 hour **serves** 4
nutritional count per serving 20.2g total fat (2.9g saturated fat); 1505kJ (360 cal); 26.6g carbohydrate; 18.3g protein; 2.1g fibre
serving suggestion Baby rocket salad.

Prawn souvlakia with tomato and fennel sauce

16 uncooked large prawns (shrimp) (1.1kg)
2 tablespoons olive oil
3 cloves garlic, crushed
2 teaspoons dried mint
1 teaspoon finely grated lemon rind
2 tablespoons lemon juice
tomato and fennel sauce
2 baby fennel (260g)
1 tablespoon olive oil
1 medium brown onion (150g), chopped finely
2 cloves garlic, chopped finely
3 medium ripe tomatoes (450g), chopped coarsely
¼ cup (60ml) ouzo or pernod
1 cup coarsely chopped fresh mint

1 Shell and devein prawns, leaving tails intact. Combine prawns in large bowl with remaining ingredients. Cover; refrigerate 1 hour.
2 Make tomato and fennel sauce.
3 Thread prawns onto eight metal skewers; reserve marinade. Cook prawns on heated oiled grill plate (or grill or barbecue or grill pan), brushing with reserved marinade, until cooked through.
4 Serve prawns with sauce.
tomato and fennel sauce Reserve fennel fronds; chop fennel and fronds finely, separately. Heat oil in medium saucepan over medium heat; cook onion, garlic and fennel until softened. Add tomato and ouzo; cook until heated through. Just before serving, stir in fronds and mint; season.

prep + cook time 35 minutes (+ refrigeration) **makes** 8
nutritional count per skewer 7.5g total fat (1.3g saturated fat); 702kJ (168 cal); 5.9g carbohydrate; 15.4g protein; 2g fibre
serving suggestion Rice pilaf.

Fish steaks with kalamata olive dressing

4 x 200g (6½-ounce) white fish steaks
2 teaspoons olive oil
1 cup coarsely chopped fresh flat-leaf parsley
kalamata olive dressing
1 medium red onion (170g), sliced thinly
1 cup (150g) seeded kalamata olives, chopped coarsely
8 anchovies (20g), drained, sliced thinly lengthways
1 tablespoon rigani
1 clove garlic, crushed
¼ cup (60ml) red wine vinegar
¼ cup (60ml) olive oil

1 Make kalamata olive dressing.
2 Brush steaks with oil; season. Cook steaks on heated grill plate (or grill or barbecue or grill pan) until cooked through.
3 Meanwhile, warm dressing in small saucepan; stir in parsley.
4 Serve steaks with dressing.
kalamata olive dressing Combine ingredients in medium bowl; season.

prep + cook time 20 minutes **serves** 4
nutritional count per serving 26g total fat (4.1g saturated fat); 1250kJ (299 cal); 2.9g carbohydrate; 13.1g protein; 2.9g fibre
tips Dressing can be made a day ahead, cover, refrigerate.
We used swordfish in this recipe; tuna steaks and firm white fish cutlets would also be fine.
serving suggestion Garlic and lemon potatoes (page 219).

Tuna souvlakia with char-grilled capsicum salad

600g (1¼-pound) piece tuna
1½ tablespoons olive oil
1 tablespoon rigani
1 teaspoon dried chilli flakes

char-grilled capsicum salad

3 medium red capsicums (bell peppers) (600g)
3 medium yellow capsicums (bell peppers) (600g)
3 cloves garlic, sliced thinly
¾ cup loosely packed fresh oregano leaves
2 tablespoons red wine vinegar

1 Cut tuna into 3cm (1¼-inch) pieces. Combine tuna, oil, rigani and chilli in medium bowl; season. Thread tuna onto eight metal skewers; place in shallow dish, cover, refrigerate 30 minutes.
2 Meanwhile, make char-grilled capsicum salad.
3 Cook tuna on heated grill plate (or grill or barbecue or grill pan), until cooked as desired.
4 Serve tuna with salad.

char-grilled capsicum salad Cook capsicums on heated grill plate (or grill or barbecue or grill pan) over high heat, turning, until skin blackens. Place capsicums in large bowl, cover with plastic; cool. Peel away skin, then slice capsicum thinly. Place capsicum in medium bowl with garlic, oregano and vinegar; toss gently to combine. Season to taste.

prep + cook time 40 minutes (+ refrigeration & cooling) **serves** 4
nutritional count per serving 9g total fat (1.4g saturated fat); 1155kJ (275 cal); 8.9g carbohydrate; 39.1g protein; 5.4g fibre

Oven-roasted fish with braised fennel

2 baby fennel bulbs (260g)
2 tablespoons olive oil
1 medium red onion (170g), cut into thin wedges
1 cup (100g) large seeded green olives
1 medium lemon (140g)
1 cup (250ml) dry white wine
½ cup (125ml) fish stock
4 x 200g (6½-ounce) skinless white fish fillets

1 Preheat oven to 180°C/350°F.
2 Remove fennel fronds from tops of bulbs; chop coarsely, reserve. Slice fennel bulbs thickly lengthways.
3 Heat half the oil in medium baking dish over heat. Cook fennel, onion and olives, stirring, until browned lightly. Remove rind from lemon with zester, add to dish with wine and stock; bring to the boil. Transfer dish to oven; cook, uncovered, about 10 minutes or until fennel is soft. Season.
4 Meanwhile, heat remaining oil in medium frying pan. Pat fish dry; season. Brown fish lightly both sides – do not cook through.
5 Increase oven to 200°C/400°F. Place fish on top of fennel mixture; cook in oven about 5 minutes or until fish is cooked through. Serve sprinkled with reserved fennel fronds.

prep + cook time 35 minutes **serves** 4
nutritional count per serving 20.8g total fat (4g saturated fat); 1620kJ (387 cal); 4.5g carbohydrate; 42g protein; 2.3g fibre
tip We used blue eye in this recipe, but any white fish fillet would be fine.

AKRO

Octopus in red wine

1.5kg (3 pounds) octopus tentacles
1½ cups (375ml) dry red wine
¼ cup (60ml) red wine vinegar
¼ cup (60ml) olive oil
2 cloves garlic, sliced thinly
2 bay leaves
1 fresh small red chilli, sliced
1 cinnamon stick
2 teaspoons whole allspice
2 strips lemon rind
1½ cups (375ml) water
12 baby brown pickling onions (240g)
8 baby chat potatoes (240g)
1 cup coarsely chopped fresh flat-leaf parsley

1 Preheat oven to 120°C/250°F.
2 Combine octopus, wine, vinegar, oil, garlic, bay leaves, chilli, cinnamon, allspice, rind and the water in large deep flameproof dish. Cook, covered, in oven 1 hour. Add onions to dish, cook, covered, about 30 minutes or until tender.
3 Remove octopus and onions from dish. Bring liquid in dish to the boil; add potatoes, simmer, uncovered, about 20 minutes or until potatoes are tender. Remove potatoes; cut in half. Simmer sauce, uncovered, about 15 minutes or until sauce is reduced to about 2 cups.
4 Meanwhile, thickly slice octopus. Add to sauce with onions and potatoes, cook until heated through. Just before serving, add parsley. Season to taste.

prep + cook time 2 hours 20 minutes **serves** 6
nutritional count per serving 11.7g total fat (2g saturated fat); 1421kJ (339 cal); 12.5g carbohydrate; 65.6g protein; 2.3g fibre
serving suggestion Crusty bread.

Prawn and zucchini with minted pilaf

20 uncooked medium prawns (shrimp) (1kg)
60g (2 ounces) butter
1 tablespoon olive oil
1 medium white onion (150g), chopped finely
2 cloves garlic, chopped finely
1 fresh small red chilli, chopped finely
1 ½ cups (300g) white long-grain rice
1 teaspoon finely grated lemon rind
¼ cup (60ml) dry white wine
1 ½ cups (375ml) hot fish stock
3 medium zucchini (360g), grated coarsely
minted lemon dressing
2 medium lemons (280g), peeled, segmented
1 cup loosely packed fresh flat-leaf parsley leaves
½ cup loosely packed fresh mint leaves
¼ cup (60ml) olive oil

1 Shell and devein prawns, leaving tails intact; refrigerate.
2 Heat butter and oil in medium heavy-based saucepan; cook onion, garlic and chilli, stirring, until onion softens. Add rice, rind and wine; cook until liquid has evaporated. Stir in hot stock, bring to the boil. Reduce heat to low, stirring; cook, covered, 10 minutes.
3 Meanwhile, make minted lemon dressing.
4 Stir zucchini into rice mixture; top with prawns. Cover; cook 5 minutes. Remove from heat; stand, covered, 5 minutes.
5 Serve pilaf drizzled with dressing.
minted lemon dressing Process ingredients until chopped finely. Season to taste.

prep + cook time 40 minutes **serves** 4
nutritional count per serving 32.3g total fat (11.2g saturated fat); 2880kJ (688 cal); 64.2g carbohydrate; 33.2g protein; 4.6g fibre

Oven-baked fish with tomato and olives

4 x 260g (8½-ounce) whole white fish
1 tablespoon olive oil
2 medium red onions (340g), sliced thinly
2 stalks celery (300g), trimmed, sliced thinly
4 cloves garlic, sliced thinly
400g (12½ ounces) cherry tomatoes
¾ cup (120g) seeded black olives
1 medium lemon (140g), halved, sliced thinly
¼ cup fresh rosemary sprigs
1 cup (250ml) dry white wine
½ cup coarsely chopped fresh flat-leaf parsley

1 Preheat oven to 200°C/400°F.
2 Remove heads from fish; clean fish.
3 Heat oil in medium baking dish; cook onion, celery and garlic, stirring, until browned lightly. Add tomatoes, olives, lemon and rosemary.
4 Season fish; place on vegetables. Pour wine over fish. Roast, uncovered, about 15 minutes or until fish is cooked through.
5 Serve fish sprinkled with parsley.

prep + cook time 40 minutes **serves** 4
nutritional count per serving 2.9g total fat (0.5g saturated fat); 253kJ (60 cal); 1.8g carbohydrate; 5.9g protein; 1.3g fibre
tip We used plate-sized leather jackets in this recipe, but any white fish would be fine.
serving suggestions Potato, pasta or rice salad.

Salmon spinach fillo parcels

500g (1 pound) spinach, trimmed
cooking-oil spray
4 sheets fillo pastry
4 x 160g (5-ounce) salmon fillets
2 cups (520g) bottled tomato pasta sauce

1 Preheat oven to 220°C/425°F. Oil oven tray; line with baking paper.
2 Boil, steam or microwave spinach until just wilted; drain. When cool enough to handle, squeeze excess liquid from spinach; chop coarsely.
3 Spray each sheet of pastry with oil. Fold each sheet in half widthways. Place one sheet on board; centre one salmon fillet on pastry, top with a quarter of the spinach. Fold in sides of pastry and roll to enclose filling. Spray parcel with oil; place on tray, seam-side down. Repeat to make three more parcels.
4 Bake parcels about 15 minutes or until pastry is browned lightly and fish is cooked through.
5 Bring sauce to the boil in small saucepan. Serve sauce with parcels.

prep + cook time 40 minutes **serves** 4
nutritional count per serving 14.8g total fat (2.9g saturated fat); 1534kJ (367 cal); 20.2g carbohydrate; 36g protein; 4.4g fibre

Fish gyros

2 tablespoons olive oil
1 tablespoon red wine vinegar
2 medium tomatoes (300g), cut into thin wedges
50g (1½ ounces) baby rocket (arugula) leaves
4 x 110g (3½-ounce) long thin white fish fillets, halved
1 tablespoon finely chopped fresh oregano
4 x 20cm (8-inch) flour tortillas
½ cup (140g) yogurt
1 clove garlic, crushed

1 Combine half the oil with vinegar, tomato and rocket in medium bowl.
2 Combine fish, oregano and remaining oil in medium bowl. Thread fish lengthways onto eight bamboo skewers. Cook skewers on heated oiled grill plate (or grill or barbecue) until cooked.
3 Wrap tortillas in foil; warm on heated grill plate about 2 minutes, turning once, or until heated through.
4 Serve warm tortillas topped with fish and salad; drizzle with combined yogurt and garlic.

prep + cook time 30 minutes **serves** 4
nutritional count per serving 15.3g total fat (3.2g saturated fat); 1417kJ (339 cal); 21g carbohydrate; 28.1g protein; 2.3g fibre
tips Soak bamboo skewers in cold water for at least an hour before using to prevent them scorching during cooking. We used flathead fillets in this recipe.

Calamari stuffed with fetta and chilli

8 whole calamari with tentacles (600g)
400g (12½ ounces) firm fetta cheese
1 teaspoon dried chilli flakes
2 tablespoons olive oil
2 tablespoons coarsely chopped fresh oregano
2 teaspoons finely grated lemon rind
2 tablespoons lemon juice
1 clove garlic, crushed
¼ cup (60ml) olive oil, extra

1 Clean calamari by pulling gently on tentacles to remove. Cut tentacles off below eyes; discard eyes, small black beak in centre of the tentacles and entrails. Remove clear quill from inside body, then remove side flaps and dark membrane. Rinse well; pat dry.
2 Mash cheese, chilli, oil and oregano together in small bowl. Spoon cheese mixture into calamari tubes; secure with toothpicks.
3 Combine calamari and tentacles in large shallow dish with rind, juice, garlic and extra oil. Cover; refrigerate 3 hours, turning occasionally.
4 Cook calamari and tentacles in heated oiled grill pan about 3 minutes each side or until browned and filling is heated through.

prep + cook time 50 minutes (+ refrigeration) **serves** 8
nutritional count per serving 23.4g total fat (9.4g saturated fat); 1116kJ (267 cal); 0.3g carbohydrate; 14.3g protein; 0.1g fibre
tip Calamari, like all seafood, cooks incredibly quickly; it's important not to overcook it because it will become tough and chewy, ruining the delicate nature of this tasty dish.
serving suggestion Tomato, capsicum and cucumber salad.

Fish and potato stew

1 cup (200g) french-style green lentils
2 tablespoons olive oil
1 medium red onion (170g), chopped finely
3 cloves garlic, crushed
2 medium potatoes (400g), chopped coarsely
1 litre (4 cups) chicken stock
4 sprigs fresh thyme
800g (1½ pounds) skinless white fish fillets, cut into 5cm (2-inch) pieces
320g (10 ounces) silver beet (swiss chard) leaves, trimmed, shredded finely

1 Cook lentils in medium saucepan of boiling water about 10 minutes or until tender; drain.
2 Meanwhile, heat oil in large saucepan; cook onion and garlic, stirring, until onion softens. Add potato, stock and thyme; bring to the boil. Reduce heat; simmer, uncovered, about 10 minutes or until potato is tender. Add lentils and fish; simmer, uncovered, about 3 minutes or until fish is cooked through.
3 Add silver beet to stew; cook, stirring, until leaves are wilted.

prep + cook time 40 minutes **serves** 4
nutritional count per serving 15.8g total fat (3.4g saturated fat); 2257kJ (540 cal); 34.8g carbohydrate; 59.1g protein; 10.3g fibre
tip We used ling fillets in this recipe.

Tomato and oregano prawns

1kg (2 pounds) uncooked medium tiger prawns (shrimp)
2 tablespoons olive oil
8 green onions (scallions), sliced thinly
4 cloves garlic, sliced thinly
½ cup (125ml) dry white wine
700g (1½ pounds) bottled tomato pasta sauce
2 tablespoons coarsely chopped fresh oregano leaves

1 Shell and devein prawns, leaving tails intact.
2 Heat oil in large frying pan; cook prawns, onion and garlic, in two batches, until prawns are changed in colour. Remove from pan; transfer to large bowl.
3 Add wine to same heated pan; simmer until liquid is reduced by half. Add pasta sauce; bring to the boil. Reduce heat; simmer, uncovered, about 5 minutes or until sauce is thickened.
4 Return prawn mixture to sauce with oregano; stir gently until prawns are heated through.

prep + cook time 30 minutes **serves** 4
nutritional count per serving 3.1g total fat (0.4g saturated fat); 364kJ (87 cal); 5g carbohydrate; 7.8g protein; 1.1g fibre
serving suggestions Orzo or risoni pasta.

Herbed fish skewers with potato smash and skordalia

800g (1½ pounds) white fish fillets, cut into 2cm (¾-inch) pieces
¼ cup (60ml) olive oil
2 tablespoons each finely chopped fresh flat-leaf parsley and lemon thyme
1kg (2 pounds) baby new potatoes, unpeeled
½ cup (120g) sour cream
40g (1½ ounces) butter, softened

skordalia

1 small potato (120g)
1 slice white bread
2 cloves garlic, crushed
1 tablespoon cider vinegar
¼ cup (60ml) water
2 tablespoons olive oil

1 Thread fish onto eight skewers; place in medium shallow dish. Brush with combined oil and herbs. Cover; refrigerate 20 minutes.
2 Meanwhile, make skordalia.
3 Boil, steam or microwave potatoes until tender; drain. Mash half the potatoes in medium bowl with sour cream and butter until smooth. Using fork, crush remaining potatoes until skins burst; fold into mash mixture. Cover to keep warm.
4 Cook skewers on heated oiled grill plate (or grill or barbecue). Serve smash with fish skewers and skordalia.
skordalia Boil, steam or microwave potato until tender; drain. Mash potato in medium bowl until smooth. Discard crusts from bread. Soak bread in small bowl of cold water; drain. Squeeze out excess liquid. Blend or process bread with remaining ingredients until smooth. Stir bread mixture into potato.

prep + cook time 50 minutes (+ refrigeration) **serves** 4
nutritional count per serving 44.7g total fat (16.7g saturated fat); 3114kJ (745 cal); 39.8g carbohydrate; 42.9g protein; 5.3g fibre
tips We used blue-eye for this recipe.
Soak bamboo skewers in water for 1 hour before using to prevent them scorching during cooking.

Salt cod and potato pie

You will need to start this recipe 24 hours ahead.

1.5kg (3 pounds) salt cod
2 tablespoons olive oil
2 medium brown onions (300g), sliced thinly
4 cloves garlic, crushed
1½ cups (300g) white long-grain rice
1 cup coarsely chopped fresh flat-leaf parsley
½ cup coarsely chopped fresh dill
8 small potatoes (800g), sliced thinly
1.5 litres (6 cups) fish stock
2 tablespoons coarsely chopped flat-leaf parsley, extra

1 Soak cod in cold water for 8 hours, changing the water twice.
2 Heat oil in large frying pan; cook onion and garlic, stirring, until onion softens. Transfer to bowl; stir in rice and herbs. Season with pepper.
3 Preheat oven to 200°C/400°F. Drain cod. Remove skin, cut cod into large pieces, discarding any bones; gently stir into rice mixture.
4 Cover base of deep 4-litre (16-cup) ovenproof dish with one-third of the potato. Top with half the fish mixture; repeat layers with remaining potato and fish mixture, ending with potato. Place dish on oven tray, pour stock into dish.
5 Bake pie, uncovered, about 1¾ hours or until potatoes are tender. Stand 10 minutes. Sprinkle with extra parsley before serving.

prep + cook time 2 hours 30 minutes (+ standing) **serves** 8
nutritional count per serving 9.9g total fat (1.5g saturated fat); 3215kJ (768 cal); 44g carbohydrate; 118g protein; 3.5g fibre
tip Salt cod is available from most Greek, Italian and Portuguese delicatessens and fishmongers.

Crisp-skinned fish with roast garlic skordalia

4 x 200g (6½-ounce) white fish fillets, skin on

rosemary oil

¼ cup (60ml) olive oil
4 cloves garlic, sliced thinly
2 tablespoons rosemary

roast garlic skordalia

2 medium bulbs garlic (140g)
600g (1¼ pounds) small potatoes
½ cup (125ml) milk, warmed
1 tablespoon finely grated lemon rind
½ cup (125ml) olive oil
½ cup (140g) greek-style yogurt
¼ cup (60ml) lemon juice

1 Make rosemary oil and roast garlic skordalia.
2 Pat fish dry with absorbent paper; season. Heat 1 tablespoon of the rosemary oil in medium frying pan; cook fish, skin-side down, about 2 minutes or until skin is crisp. Turn fish, cook fish through.
3 Serve fish with skordalia, drizzled with rosemary oil.

rosemary oil Heat oil, garlic and rosemary in small saucepan over low heat until garlic begins to colour. Cool.

roast garlic skordalia Preheat oven to 220°C/425°F. Wrap garlic in foil; place on oven tray with potatoes. Roast about 30 minutes or until garlic and potatoes are soft. Stand until cool enough to handle. Peel potatoes; place flesh in medium bowl. Squeeze garlic from cloves, add to potatoes with half the warm milk. Mash rind, garlic and potatoes until smooth. Gradually stir in oil, 1 tablespoon at a time. Stir in yogurt and juice; season to taste. Just before serving, heat remaining milk in medium saucepan; add skordalia, cook, stirring, until heated through.

prep + cook time 1 hour (+ cooling) **serves** 4
nutritional count per serving 53.4g total fat (11g saturated fat); 3210kJ (767 cal); 24g carbohydrate; 47.7g protein; 6.7g fibre
tip We used barramundi in this recipe, but any white fish fillets would be fine.

Salt-baked whole snapper with fennel and mint salad

1.5kg (3-pound) whole snapper
1 large fennel bulb (300g)
1 medium lemon (140g), sliced thinly
5 sprigs fresh thyme
3kg (6 pounds) coarse cooking salt
8 egg whites

fennel and mint salad
2 medium zucchini (240g)
1 cup loosely packed fresh mint leaves
¼ cup (60ml) olive oil
2 tablespoons red wine vinegar

1 Preheat oven to 220°C/425°F. Line large baking dish with baking paper.
2 Clean fish, leave scales intact. Pat fish dry inside and out with absorbent paper. Season fish cavity. Remove stems from fennel. Fill fish cavity with lemon, thyme and fennel stems.
3 Combine salt and egg whites in large bowl. Spread half the mixture over base of dish, top with fish, then pack remaining salt mixture over fish to cover completely – the tail can be left out, if you like.
4 Bake fish about 35 minutes or until a skewer inserted into thickest part of fish feels hot when withdrawn. Stand fish 10 minutes before cracking the salt crust open.
5 Meanwhile, make fennel and mint salad.
6 Serve fish with salad.

fennel and mint salad Thinly shave fennel bulb lengthways; place in bowl of iced water. Using vegetable peeler, slice zucchini lengthways into ribbons. Combine zucchini and mint in bowl. Drain fennel, add to zucchini mixture with coarsely chopped fennel fronds, oil and vinegar; season to taste.

prep + cook time 1 hour **serves** 4
nutritional count per serving 21.3g total fat (4.2g saturated fat); 1540kJ (368 cal); 2.5g carbohydrate; 41g protein; 1.9g fibre
tip Use a mandolin or V-slicer to shave the fennel bulb for best results.

LAMB + GOAT

Baked lamb shanks with orzo

1 tablespoon olive oil
4 french-trimmed lamb shanks (1kg)
1 medium brown onion (150g), chopped finely
3 cinnamon sticks
1 bay leaf
3 cloves garlic, crushed
400g (12½ ounces) canned diced tomatoes
2 cups (500ml) chicken stock
1¼ cups (275g) orzo (pasta)
1 cup (250ml) water
2 tablespoons fresh oregano leaves

1 Preheat oven to 200°C/400°F.
2 Heat oil in large baking dish; cook lamb over medium heat until browned all over. Remove from dish.
3 Cook onion, cinnamon and bay leaf in same dish, stirring, until onion softens. Add garlic; cook, stirring, until fragrant. Return lamb to dish with undrained tomatoes and stock; bring to the boil. Cover dish with lid or foil; cook in oven 1¼ hours.
4 Stir orzo and the water into dish; cook, covered, about 30 minutes or until lamb and orzo are tender. Season to taste.
5 Serve lamb sprinkled with oregano.

prep + cook time 2 hours 10 minutes **serves** 4
nutritional count per serving 14g total fat (4.2g saturated fat); 2045kJ (488 cal); 53.8g carbohydrate; 35.9g protein; 4.6g fibre
tip You can replace orzo with risoni if you like. Orzo, like risoni, absorbs cooking liquid. If the sauce is too thick, stir in a little extra water. If you make this dish in advance, you will need to add some water or stock when reheating.

Moussaka

¼ cup (60ml) olive oil
2 large eggplants (1kg), sliced thinly
1 large brown onion (200g), chopped finely
2 cloves garlic, crushed
1kg (2 pounds) minced (ground) lamb
410g (13 ounces) canned crushed tomatoes
½ cup (125ml) dry white wine
1 teaspoon ground cinnamon
¼ cup (20g) finely grated kefalotyri cheese
white sauce
75g (2½ ounces) butter
⅓ cup (50g) plain (all-purpose) flour
2 cups (500ml) milk

1 Heat oil in large frying pan; cook eggplant, in batches, until browned both sides. Drain on absorbent paper.
2 Cook onion and garlic in same pan, stirring, until onion softens. Add lamb; cook, stirring, until lamb changes colour. Stir in undrained tomatoes, wine and cinnamon; bring to the boil. Reduce heat; simmer, uncovered, about 30 minutes or until liquid has evaporated.
3 Meanwhile, preheat oven to 180°C/350°F. Oil shallow 2-litre (8-cup) rectangular baking dish.
4 Make white sauce.
5 Place one-third of the eggplant, overlapping slices slightly, in dish; spread half the meat sauce over eggplant. Repeat layering with another third of the eggplant, remaining meat sauce and remaining eggplant. Spread white sauce over top layer of eggplant; sprinkle with cheese.
6 Bake moussaka about 40 minutes or until top browns lightly. Cover; stand 10 minutes before serving.
white sauce Melt butter in medium saucepan, add flour; cook, stirring, until mixture bubbles and thickens. Gradually add milk; stir until mixture boils and thickens.

prep + cook time 1 hour 50 minutes **serves** 6
nutritional count per serving 36.6g total fat (16.5g saturated fat); 2420kJ (579 cal); 18g carbohydrate; 41.8g protein; 5.3g fibre
serving suggestion Green salad.

Pastitsio

250g (8 ounces) macaroni pasta
2 eggs, beaten lightly
¾ cup (60g) coarsely grated kefalotyri cheese
2 tablespoons fresh breadcrumbs

meat sauce
2 tablespoons olive oil
2 medium brown onions (300g), chopped finely
750g (1½ pounds) minced (ground) lamb
410g (13 ounces) canned crushed tomatoes
⅓ cup (90g) tomato paste
½ cup (125ml) beef stock
¼ cup (60ml) dry white wine
½ teaspoon ground cinnamon
1 egg, beaten lightly

cheese sauce
90g (3 ounces) butter
½ cup (75g) plain (all-purpose) flour
3½ cups (875ml) milk
1 cup (80g) coarsely grated kefalotyri cheese
2 egg yolks

1 Preheat oven to 180°C/350°F. Oil shallow 2.5-litre (10-cup) ovenproof dish.
2 Make meat sauce and cheese sauce.
3 Cook pasta in large saucepan of boiling water until tender; drain. Combine hot pasta, egg and cheese in large bowl. Press pasta over base of dish.
4 Top pasta evenly with meat sauce; pour over cheese sauce. Smooth surface; sprinkle with breadcrumbs.
5 Bake pastitsio about 1 hour or until browned lightly. Stand 10 minutes before serving.

meat sauce Heat oil in large saucepan; cook onion and lamb, stirring, until lamb is browned. Stir in tomato, paste, stock, wine and cinnamon; simmer, uncovered, 20 minutes or until mixture is thick. Cool; stir in egg.

cheese sauce Melt butter in medium saucepan, add flour; cook, stirring, until mixture bubbles and thickens. Remove from heat; gradually stir in milk. Stir over heat until sauce boils and thickens; stir in cheese. Cool 5 minutes; stir in egg yolks.

prep + cook time 2 hours 15 minutes **serves** 6
nutritional count per serving 45.8g total fat (23.2g saturated fat); 3440kJ (823 cal); 51.6g carbohydrate; 48.4g protein; 4g fibre

Slow-roasted lamb with skordalia and potatoes

2kg (4-pound) leg of lamb
2 cloves garlic, crushed
½ cup (125ml) lemon juice
2 tablespoons olive oil
1 tablespoon fresh oregano leaves
2 teaspoons fresh lemon thyme leaves
5 large potatoes (1.5kg), chopped coarsely
1 tablespoon finely grated lemon rind
2 tablespoons lemon juice, extra
2 tablespoons olive oil, extra

skordalia
1 medium potato (200g), quartered
3 cloves garlic, crushed
1 tablespoon lemon juice
1 tablespoon white wine vinegar
2 tablespoons water
⅓ cup (80ml) olive oil

1 Combine lamb, garlic, juice, oil, oregano and half the thyme in large bowl. Cover; refrigerate 3 hours or overnight.
2 Preheat oven to 160°C/325°F.
3 Place lamb mixture in large baking dish; roast, uncovered, 3 hours.
4 Meanwhile, make skordalia.
5 Combine potatoes, rind, extra juice, extra oil and remaining thyme in large bowl. Place potatoes, in single layer, on oven tray. Roast potatoes, uncovered, for last 30 minutes of lamb cooking time.
6 Remove lamb from oven; cover to keep warm.
7 Increase oven to 220°C/425°F; roast potatoes a further 20 minutes or until browned lightly and cooked through.
8 Serve potatoes and lamb with skordalia and pan juices.
skordalia Boil, steam or microwave potato until tender; drain. Push potato through fine sieve into medium bowl; cool 10 minutes. Whisk combined garlic, juice, vinegar and the water into potato. Gradually whisk in oil in a thin, steady stream; continue whisking until skordalia thickens. Stir in about a tablespoon of warm water if skordalia becomes too thick.

prep + cook time 4 hours (+ refrigeration) **serves** 4
nutritional count per serving 57g total fat (14g saturated fat); 4556kJ (1090 cal); 51.5g carbohydrate; 91.2g protein; 6.7g fibre

Lemon and garlic lamb kebabs

8 x 15cm (6-inch) stalks fresh rosemary
750g (1 ½ pounds) lamb fillets, cut into 3cm (1 ¼-inch) pieces
3 cloves garlic, crushed
2 tablespoons olive oil
2 teaspoons finely grated lemon rind
1 tablespoon lemon juice

1 Remove leaves from bottom two-thirds of each rosemary stalk; sharpen trimmed ends to a point.
2 Thread lamb onto rosemary skewers. Brush kebabs with combined garlic, oil, rind and juice. Cover; refrigerate until required.
3 Cook kebabs on heated oiled grill plate (or grill or barbecue), brushing frequently with remaining garlic mixture, until cooked.
4 Serve kebabs with a greek salad, if you like.

prep + cook time 30 minutes **serves** 4
nutritional count per serving 15.9g total fat (4.3g saturated fat); 1250kJ (299 cal); 0.4g carbohydrate; 38.6g protein; 0.4g fibre

Lamb meatballs with egg-lemon sauce

1 tablespoon olive oil
1 medium brown onion (150g), chopped finely
1 cup (250ml) chicken stock
500g (1 pound) spinach, trimmed, shredded
2 eggs
1½ tablespoons plain (all-purpose) flour
⅓ cup (80ml) lemon juice

meatballs

500g (1 pound) minced (ground) lamb
½ cup (35g) stale breadcrumbs
½ cup (40g) grated kefalograviera cheese
1 tablespoon finely chopped fresh dill
1 egg
2 teaspoons finely grated lemon rind

1 Make meatballs.

2 Heat oil in deep frying pan; cook meatballs until browned. Remove from pan.

3 Cook onion in same pan, stirring, until softened. Return meatballs to pan with stock; bring to the boil. Reduce heat; simmer, covered, about 15 minutes or until meatballs are cooked through. Reserve ½ cup of hot cooking liquid. Stir spinach into pan, cook until wilted. Remove pan from heat.

4 Meanwhile, beat eggs with fork in medium bowl until combined; whisk in flour and juice. Whisk in reserved hot liquid; stir mixture into meatballs. Stir gently until mixture simmers; season to taste.

meatballs Combine ingredients in large bowl; season. Roll rounded tablespoons of mixture into balls.

prep + cook time 45 minutes **serves** 4
nutritional count per serving 28.9g total fat (10.6g saturated fat); 1897kJ (453 cal); 10.6g carbohydrate; 38.4g protein; 2.4g fibre
serving suggestions Rocket (arugala) salad and crusty bread.

Seasoned rolled lamb shoulder with fetta and mint

1 medium lemon (140g)
1.4kg (2¾-pound) boned lamb shoulder
2 cloves garlic, bruised
2 tablespoons fresh oregano leaves
2 tablespoons olive oil
100g (3 ounces) fetta cheese
½ cup (35g) stale breadcrumbs
3 green onions (scallions), chopped finely
2 tablespoons finely chopped fresh mint

1 Using a vegetable peeler, peel rind thinly from lemon, avoiding white pith. Squeeze juice from lemon; reserve 1 tablespoon juice. Combine lamb, garlic, oregano, rind and oil in large bowl; turn to coat. Season with pepper. Cover, refrigerate 4 hours or overnight.
2 Combine fetta, breadcrumbs, onion, mint and reserved juice in medium bowl.
3 Preheat oven to 240°C/450°F.
4 Place rind and garlic from marinade in baking dish. Open lamb out on board, cut-side up. Spread lamb with fetta mixture; roll to enclose filling. Tie lamb at intervals with kitchen string; season.
5 Place lamb in baking dish; roast, uncovered, 20 minutes. Reduce oven to 200°C/400°F; roast, uncovered, about 40 minutes. Stand lamb, covered, 15 minutes before slicing.

prep + cook time 1 hour 25 minutes (+ refrigeration & standing)
serves 6
nutritional count per serving 29.1g total fat (10.5g saturated fat); 2030kJ (485 cal); 2.9g carbohydrate; 53g.1 protein; 0.4g fibre
serving suggestion Roast potatoes.

Roast leg of lamb with potatoes and artichokes

1.2kg (2½-pound) leg of lamb
2 cloves garlic, sliced
6 small unpeeled potatoes (720g), quartered
1 medium lemon (140g), quartered
3 sprigs fresh thyme
1½ tablespoons olive oil
400g (12½ ounces) canned artichokes in brine, drained

1 Preheat oven to 240°C/450°F.
2 Pierce lamb all over with small sharp knife; press garlic into cuts.
3 Place lamb in large baking dish. Place potatoes, lemon and thyme in single layer around lamb; season. Rub oil over lamb and potatoes. Roast, uncovered, 20 minutes. Reduce oven to 200°C/400°F; roast, uncovered, about 30 minutes or until lamb is cooked as desired. Remove lamb from dish; stand, covered, 15 minutes.
4 Meanwhile, increase oven to 220°C/425°F. Add artichokes to dish; roast, uncovered,15 minutes.
5 Serve lamb sliced with potatoes and artichokes.

prep + cook time 1 hour 25 minutes **serves** 4
nutritional count per serving 23g total fat (7g saturated fat); 2145kJ (512 cal); 24.4g carbohydrate; 51.8g protein; 9.7g fibre
tip For this cooking time, the lamb will be pink. If you prefer it well done, roast a further 20 minutes at 200°C/400°F.

Lamb fillo pie

¼ cup (60ml) olive oil
1 medium brown onion (150g), chopped finely
375g (12 ounces) minced (ground) lamb
3 cloves garlic, crushed
½ cup (125ml) dry red wine
2 tablespoons tomato paste
1 large potato (300g), chopped finely
1 cup (80g) coarsely grated kefalograviera cheese
2 tablespoons each finely chopped fresh mint and fresh oregano
15 sheets fillo pastry

1 Heat 1 tablespoon of the oil in large frying pan; cook onion, stirring, until softened. Add lamb; cook, stirring, until browned. Stir in garlic until fragrant. Add wine, paste and potato; simmer, covered, about 10 minutes or until potato is tender. Stir in cheese and herbs; season to taste.
2 Meanwhile, preheat oven to 220°C/425°F. Oil medium shallow ovenproof dish.
3 Brush 1 sheet of pastry with some of the remaining oil; top with 4 more sheets, brushing each with more oil. Line pan with pastry. Repeat with another 5 sheets of pastry, to line the opposite sides of the pan.
4 Spoon lamb mixture into pan. Layer remaining pastry sheets, brushing each with more oil; fold in half crossways. Cut to fit top of pan. Place on top of filling; fold in overhanging pastry to enclose filling.
5 Bake pie about 20 minutes or until browned.

prep + cook time 1 hour **serves** 4
nutritional count per serving 33g total fat (11g saturated fat); 2580kJ (616 cal); 43.4g carbohydrate; 33.3g protein; 4g fibre
tip When working with the first five sheets of pastry, cover remaining pastry with a sheet of baking paper then a damp tea towel to prevent it drying out.
serving suggestions Salad and yogurt.

Lamb shanks with lentils

1 tablespoon olive oil
6 french-trimmed lamb shanks (1.5kg)
1 large brown onion (200g), chopped finely
2 stalks celery (300g), trimmed, chopped finely
1 medium carrot (120g), sliced finely
2 bay leaves
3 cups (750ml) chicken stock
1 cup (250ml) water
1¼ cups (250g) brown lentils, rinsed, drained
2 tablespoons lemon juice
2 tablespoons coarsely chopped fresh flat-leaf parsley

1 Heat oil in large saucepan; cook lamb, in batches, until browned. Remove from pan.
2 Add onion, celery, carrot and bay leaves to pan; cook, stirring, about 5 minutes or until onion softens.
3 Return lamb to pan with stock and the water; bring to the boil. Reduce heat; simmer, covered, 1 hour. Stir in lentils; bring to the boil. Reduce heat; simmer, covered, 30 minutes. Uncover; simmer further 30 minutes or until lamb and lentils are tender.
4 Stir in juice and parsley; season to taste.

prep + cook time 2 hours 30 minutes **serves** 6
nutritional count per serving 12.1g total fat (4.3g saturated fat); 1547kJ (370 cal); 20.8g carbohydrate; 41.5g protein; 7.4g fibre
serving suggestion Rocket (arugula) salad.

Goat and capsicum stew

¼ cup (60ml) olive oil
1.6kg (3¼-pound) boneless goat shoulder, chopped coarsely
2 medium brown onions (300g), sliced thinly
1 bay leaf
400g (12½ ounces) canned diced tomatoes
½ cup (125ml) chicken stock
2 teaspoons rigani
2 medium red capsicums (bell peppers) (400g), sliced thinly
1 medium yellow capsicum (bell pepper) (200g), sliced thinly
2 tablespoons coarsely chopped flat leaf parsley

1 Heat 2 tablespoons of the oil in large saucepan; cook goat, in batches, until browned. Remove from pan.
2 Heat remaining oil in same pan; cook onion and bay leaf, stirring, until onion softens. Return goat to pan with undrained tomatoes, stock and rigani; bring to the boil. Reduce heat; simmer, covered, 2½ hours.
3 Stir in capsicum; simmer, covered, about 20 minutes or until capsicum is tender. Season to taste. Serve sprinkled with parsley.

prep + cook time 3 hours 15 minutes **serves** 6
nutritional count per serving 17.5g total fat (4.1g saturated fat); 2105kJ (503 cal); 6.9g carbohydrate; 74.5g protein; 3.3g fibre
tip Goat shoulder is good for stews and casseroles as it needs long slow cooking to be tender. It is sold in Greek and specialty butchers and often comes frozen. Ask the butcher to cut the meat into chunks while frozen and thaw meat in refrigerator at home.
serving suggestions Rice or mashed potatoes.

Goat kleftiko

1.5kg (3-pound) goat shoulder
3 cloves garlic, sliced
2 tablespoons olive oil
¼ cup coarsely chopped fresh oregano
1 tablespoon finely grated lemon rind
2 tablespoons lemon juice
90g (3 ounces) kefalograviera cheese, sliced thickly

1 Preheat oven to 170°C/340°F.
2 Pierce goat all over with small sharp knife, press garlic into cuts; season. Heat oil in large frying pan; cook goat until browned.
3 Layer two sheets of baking paper; fold into quarters then open. Place paper in large baking dish; place goat in centre of creases. Sprinkle goat with oregano and rind; drizzle with juice. Top with cheese; fold paper over to enclose, sealing edges to avoid juices escaping. Wrap in foil.
4 Roast goat about 2½ hours or until goat is tender. Stand 15 minutes before serving.

prep + cook time 3 hours (+ standing) **serves** 4
nutritional count per serving 10.5g total fat (3.6g saturated fat); 1045kJ (250 cal); 0.4g carbohydrate; 36.3g protein; 0.3g fibre
tips Goat is sold in Greek and specialty butchers and often comes frozen. The leg of goat will give more meat than the shoulder and will take up to 4 hours to roast.
The name kleftiko comes from the "klephts", bandits who used to roam the Greek countryside, stealing goats and lambs and then cooking them in a sealed pit to avoid any smoke being seen. Nowadays, the meat is cooked in a parcel or in a clay pot dish. This method ensures that all the juices and moisture remain and the meat falls off the bone.
serving suggestions Pan-fried potatoes and salad.

Stuffed eggplant with lamb and rice

2 large eggplants (1kg), halved
¼ cup (60ml) olive oil
1 medium brown onion (150g), chopped finely
300g (9½ ounces) minced (ground) lamb
3 cloves garlic, crushed
⅓ cup (65g) medium-grain rice
½ cup (125ml) water
1 tablespoon lemon juice
2 teaspoons rigani
⅔ cup (50g) coarsely grated kefalograviera cheese

1 Preheat oven to 220°C/425°F.
2 Cut a 1cm (½-inch) border inside each eggplant; scoop out flesh without breaking skin. Place eggplant shells on oven tray; brush with 1 tablespoon of the oil. Roast about 20 minutes or until tender.
3 Meanwhile, coarsely chop eggplant flesh. Heat 1 tablespoon of the oil in medium frying pan; cook eggplant, stirring, until tender. Remove from pan.
4 Heat remaining oil in same pan; cook onion, stirring, until softened. Add lamb; cook, stirring, until browned. Add garlic, cook, stirring, until fragrant. Return eggplant to pan with rice and the water; cook, covered, over low heat, about 10 minutes or until rice is tender. Stir in juice and rigani; season to taste.
5 Spoon lamb mixture into eggplant shells; sprinkle with cheese. Roast about 20 minutes or until cheese is browned.

prep + cook time 1 hour **serves** 4
nutritional count per serving 28.4g total fat (8.5g saturated fat); 1800kJ (430 cal); 20.5g carbohydrate; 23.6g protein; 7.2g fibre
serving suggestion Greek salad.

Barbecued lamb sandwiches

1 medium lemon (140g)
900g (1¾-pound) boneless lamb shoulder
3 cloves garlic, crushed
2 tablespoons fresh oregano leaves
2 sprigs fresh thyme
2 tablespoons olive oil
¼ medium iceberg lettuce, shredded thinly
2 medium tomatoes (300g), sliced thinly
1 small red onion (100g), sliced thinly
1 cup (140g) tzatziki
6 large pitta breads (480g), toasted lightly

1 Using a vegetable peeler, peel rind thinly from lemon, avoiding white pith. Combine lamb, rind, garlic, herbs and oil in shallow dish; cover, refrigerate 4 hours. Drain lamb; season.
2 Heat grill plate (or grill or barbecue or grill pan); cook lamb, covered, about 25 minutes, turning halfway through. Stand, loosely covered with foil, 15 minutes before slicing.
3 Serve lamb with lettuce, tomato, onion, tzatziki on warmed pitta bread.

prep + cook time 1 hour (+ refrigeration & standing) **serves** 6
nutritional count per serving 18.8g total fat (5.5g saturated fat); 2064kJ (493 cal); 44.8g carbohydrate; 36.3g protein; 4.9g fibre
tips This is a homemade version of the Greek sandwich, called gyros. Gyros are made from slices of meat cooked on a turning spit.
You can make your own tzatziki (page 31) for this recipe, if you like.

Lamb cutlets with spinach skordalia

2 tablespoons olive oil
2 tablespoons lemon juice
2 cloves garlic, crushed
2 teaspoons rigani
18 french-trimmed small lamb cutlets (900g)
spinach skordalia
⅓ cup (80ml) water
¾ cup (50g) fresh breadcrumbs
1kg (2 pounds) spinach, trimmed, chopped coarsely
¾ cup (75g) roasted walnuts
2 cloves garlic, chopped coarsely
¼ cup (60ml) lemon juice
¼ cup (60ml) olive oil

1 Combine oil, juice, garlic and rigani with lamb in large bowl. Cover; refrigerate 1 hour.
2 Meanwhile, make spinach skordalia.
3 Cook lamb, in batches, on heated oiled grill plate (or grill or barbecue) until browned both sides and cooked as desired.
4 Serve cutlets with skordalia.
spinach skordalia Combine the water and breadcrumbs in small bowl. Boil, steam or microwave spinach until just wilted; drain. When cool enough to handle, squeeze excess liquid from spinach. Blend or process spinach and breadcrumb mixture with nuts, garlic and juice until smooth. With motor operating, gradually add oil in a thin steady stream; process until skordalia thickens.

prep + cook time 30 minutes (+ refrigeration) **serves** 6
nutritional count per serving 37.5g total fat (8.6g saturated fat); 1944kJ (465 cal); 7.7g carbohydrate; 22.3g protein; 6g fibre
tip If you don't have much time, don't worry about marinating the lamb – just brush both sides of the cutlets with the lemon mixture. If you do this, make the skordalia first.

Braised lamb shanks with white bean puree

1 tablespoon olive oil
8 french-trimmed lamb shanks (2kg)
1 large red onion (300g), chopped
2 cloves garlic, crushed
1 cup (250ml) chicken stock
2 cups (500ml) water
400g (12½ ounces) canned diced tomatoes
1 tablespoon fresh rosemary leaves
4 drained anchovy fillets, chopped
2 large red capsicums (bell peppers) (700g)
2 large green capsicums (bell peppers) (700g)

white bean puree
20g (¾ ounce) butter
1 small brown onion (80g), chopped finely
1 clove garlic, crushed
¼ cup (60ml) dry white wine
¾ cup (180ml) chicken stock
2 x 400g (12½ ounces) canned white beans, rinsed, drained
2 tablespoons pouring cream

1 Heat oil in large deep saucepan; cook lamb, in batches, until browned all over. Remove from pan.
2 Cook onion and garlic in same pan, stirring, until onion softens. Add stock, the water, undrained tomatoes, rosemary and anchovy; bring to the boil. Return lamb to pan, reduce heat; simmer, covered, 1 hour, stirring occasionally. Uncover; simmer about 45 minutes or until lamb is tender.
3 Meanwhile, quarter capsicums; discard seeds and membranes. Roast under hot grill or in very hot oven, skin-side up, until skin blisters and blackens. Cover capsicum pieces with plastic wrap or paper for 5 minutes; peel away skin, slice capsicum thickly.
4 Meanwhile, make white bean puree.
5 Add capsicum to lamb; cook, uncovered, 5 minutes. Serve lamb on white bean puree.
white bean puree Melt butter in medium frying pan; cook onion and garlic, stirring, until onions softens. Add wine; cook, stirring, until liquid is reduced by half. Add stock and beans; bring to the boil. Reduce heat; simmer, uncovered, about 10 minutes or until liquid is almost evaporated. Blend or process bean mixture and cream until smooth.

prep + cook time 3 hours 10 minutes **serves** 4
nutritional count per serving 18.8g total fat (8.4g saturated fat); 2312kJ (553 cal); 21g carbohydrate; 72.1g protein; 8.6g fibre

Lamb and okra in rich tomato sauce with garlic confit

1 tablespoon olive oil
1kg (2-pound) boneless lamb shoulder, trimmed, chopped coarsely
2 medium brown onions (300g), chopped coarsely
7 medium tomatoes (1kg), chopped coarsely
1 litre (4 cups) water
200g (6½ ounces) okra
½ cup loosely packed fresh mint leaves

garlic confit
1 teaspoon coriander seeds
½ teaspoon cardamom seeds
30g (1 ounce) butter
5 cloves garlic, sliced thinly
1 teaspoon dried chilli flakes
1 teaspoon salt

1 Heat oil in large deep saucepan; cook lamb, in batches, until browned all over. Remove from pan.
2 Cook onion in same pan, stirring, until soft. Add tomato and the water; bring to the boil. Return lamb to pan, reduce heat; simmer, uncovered, stirring occasionally, about 1¾ hours or until lamb is tender.
3 Add okra to lamb mixture; simmer, uncovered, about 15 minutes or until okra is tender.
4 Meanwhile, make garlic confit.
5 Serve casserole with garlic confit and mint.
garlic confit Using mortar and pestle, crush seeds. Melt butter in small saucepan; cook seeds, garlic, chilli and salt over low heat, stirring, about 10 minutes or until garlic softens.

prep + cook time 2 hours 30 minutes **serves** 4
nutritional count per serving 33.5g total fat (15g saturated fat); 2286kJ (547 cal); 8g carbohydrate; 53.4g protein; 6.4g fibre
tip Confit is a preserved food item, usually meat like duck, goose or pork. Salted and cooked slowly in its own fat, the meat is packed into a dish and covered with the cooking mixture, which seals and preserves it. The word confit is also used to describe a cooking method that results in the preservation of a particular ingredient, such as garlic or lemons.
serving suggestion Steamed white rice.

Layered vine leaves, eggplant and lamb

2 large red capsicums (bell peppers) (700g)
1 medium eggplant (300g), cut crossways into 12 slices
1 medium brown onion (150g), chopped finely
1 clove garlic, crushed
500g (1 pound) minced (ground) lamb
2 teaspoons baharat
1 tablespoon brandy
1 tablespoon tomato paste
½ cup (125ml) beef stock
1 tablespoon lime juice
1 tablespoon roasted pine nuts
1 cup coarsely chopped fresh flat-leaf parsley
8 fresh vine leaves

1 Quarter capsicums; discard seeds and membrane. Place capsicum, skin-side up, and eggplant on oiled oven tray under hot grill or in hot oven until skin blisters. Cover capsicum with plastic wrap or paper 5 minutes; peel away skin, then slice thinly.
2 Meanwhile, cook onion and garlic in heated oiled large frying pan, stirring, until onion just softens. Add lamb and spice; cook, stirring, until lamb changes colour. Stir in combined brandy, paste and stock; bring to the boil. Reduce heat; simmer, uncovered, stirring, 2 minutes or until liquid reduces by half. Remove from heat; stir in juice, nuts and parsley. Cover to keep warm.
3 Place vine leaves in large saucepan of boiling water, uncovered, about 30 seconds or until just pliable; drain, in single layer, on absorbent paper.
4 Place one leaf on each plate; layer each leaf with one slice of eggplant, a few capsicum slices, ¼ cup lamb mixture and another vine leaf. Repeat layering with remaining eggplant, capsicum and lamb mixture.

prep + cook time 40 minutes **serves** 4
nutritional count per serving 15.5g total fat (5.9g saturated fat); 1321kJ (316 cal); 10.4g carbohydrate; 31.1g protein; 5.6g fibre
tip Baharat is an Arab spice mix which usually contains allspice, black pepper, cardamom, cloves, dried coriander, cumin, nutmeg and chilli.

Lamb, fetta and spinach fillo parcels

1 kg (2 pounds) spinach, trimmed
150g (4½ ounces) fetta cheese, crumbled
1 tablespoon fresh oregano leaves
½ teaspoon cracked black pepper
1 teaspoon finely grated lemon rind
8 x 100g (3-ounce) lamb fillets
8 sheets fillo pastry
cooking-oil spray

1 Preheat oven to 240°C/450°F. Oil oven tray; line with baking paper.
2 Boil, steam or microwave spinach until just wilted; drain. When cool enough to handle, squeeze excess liquid from spinach. Chop spinach coarsely; combine in medium bowl with cheese, oregano, pepper and rind.
3 Cook lamb, in batches, in heated oiled large frying pan until browned. Remove from pan.
4 Stack 4 sheets of pastry, spraying each sheet lightly with oil. Cut fillo stack in half widthways; cover with a slightly damp tea towel to prevent drying out. Repeat process with remaining sheets of pastry.
5 Uncover one pastry stack; place on board. Centre two fillets on stack, top fillets with a quarter of the spinach mixture. Roll stack to enclose filling, folding in sides after first complete turn of roll. Spray parcel with oil; place on tray. Repeat process with remaining fillo stacks, lamb and spinach mixture.
6 Bake parcels about 15 minutes or until browned lightly.

prep + cook time 50 minutes **serves** 4
nutritional count per serving 19.5g total fat (9.3g saturated fat); 1990kJ (476 cal); 20.5g carbohydrate; 53.1g protein; 3g fibre
serving suggestions Yogurt and lemon wedges.

Lamb patties with beetroot and tzatziki

500g (1 pound) minced (ground) lamb
1 medium carrot (120g), grated coarsely
1 small brown onion (80g), chopped finely
1 egg, beaten lightly
1 clove garlic, crushed
2 tablespoons finely chopped fresh flat-leaf parsley
1 teaspoon grated lemon rind
½ teaspoon rigani
1 large turkish bread (430g)
4 outer cos lettuce leaves, shredded
400g (12½ ounces) canned whole baby beetroot, drained, quartered
tzatziki
½ cup (140g) yogurt
1 clove garlic, crushed
1 lebanese cucumber (130g), seeded, chopped finely
1 tablespoon chopped fresh mint

1 Combine lamb, carrot, onion, egg, garlic, parsley, rind and rigani in large bowl; mix well. Shape mixture into eight patties.
2 Cook patties on heated, oiled grill plate (or grill or barbecue), in batches, until browned and cooked through. Remove from grill plate.
3 Meanwhile, make tzatziki.
4 Cut bread into four equal pieces, split each piece in half crossways; toast, cut-side up, until browned lightly.
5 Just before serving, sandwich bread equally with lettuce, patties, tzatziki and beetroot.
tzatziki Combine ingredients in small bowl.

prep + cook time 30 minutes **serves** 4
nutritional count per serving 14.9g total fat (5.9g saturated fat); 2261kJ (541 cal); 61g carbohydrate; 40.1g protein; 7.2g fibre
tip The patties and tzatziki can be made several hours ahead; keep covered, separately, in the refrigerator.
serving suggestion Lemon wedges.

Lamb fritters with spicy yogurt

2 teaspoons ground cumin
1 cup (280g) yogurt
1 egg
1¾ cups (260g) self-raising flour
1½ cups (375ml) buttermilk
150g (4½ ounces) piece pumpkin, grated finely
2 green onions (scallions), chopped finely
300g (9½ ounces) leftover roast lamb, chopped coarsely
vegetable oil, for shallow-frying

1 Dry-fry cumin in large frying pan, stirring, until fragrant.
2 Combine yogurt with half the cumin in small bowl.
3 Combine egg, flour and buttermilk in large bowl with pumpkin, onion, lamb and remaining cumin.
4 Heat oil in same pan; shallow-fry ¼ cup of batter for each fritter, in batches, until fritters are browned lightly. Drain on absorbent paper. Serve fritters with yogurt.

prep + cook time 30 minutes **serves** 4
nutritional count per serving 49.2g total fat (13.3g saturated fat); 3511kJ (840 cal); 60.3g carbohydrate; 37.6g protein; 3g fibre
tips Leftover roast chicken can be used in place of the lamb in this recipe. Tarragon marries beautifully with chicken, so instead of using ground cumin, add 2 teaspoons finely chopped fresh tarragon to the batter.

Lemon-pepper lamb with minted broad bean risoni

1 tablespoon finely grated lemon rind
1 tablespoon cracked black pepper
2 teaspoons sea salt
1 clove garlic, sliced thinly
2 tablespoons olive oil
4 lamb backstraps (800g)
500g (1 pound) frozen broad (fava) beans
¾ cup (165g) risoni
4 green onions (scallions), sliced thinly
⅔ cup coarsely chopped fresh flat-leaf parsley
½ cup coarsely chopped fresh mint
2 tablespoons lemon juice

1 Combine rind, pepper, salt, garlic, half of the oil and lamb in large bowl. Cover; refrigerate 1 hour.
2 Meanwhile, place beans in large saucepan of boiling water; return to the boil. Drain; cool in iced water. Drain; discard skin.
3 Cook risoni in large saucepan of boiling water until just tender; drain. Rinse under cold water; drain.
4 Meanwhile, heat remaining oil in large non-stick frying pan; cook lamb, uncovered, until cooked as desired. Cover lamb, stand 5 minutes; slice lamb thickly.
5 Cook onion in same pan, stirring, until onion softens. Add risoni and beans; cook, stirring, until hot. Remove from heat; stir in herbs and juice. Serve broad bean risoni with lamb.

prep + cook time 55 minutes (+ refrigeration) **serves** 4
nutritional count per serving 17.2g total fat (4.6g saturated fat); 2190kJ (524 cal); 37.4g carbohydrate; 53.6g protein; 10.4g fibre

Goat and haricot bean casserole

2 cups (400g) dried haricot beans
¼ cup (60ml) olive oil
2kg (4-pound) leg of goat, boned
2 medium onions (300g), chopped finely
2 cloves garlic, crushed
2 x 425g (13½ ounces) canned crushed tomatoes
½ cup (125ml) dry red wine
¼ cup (60ml) tomato paste
1 cinnamon stick
1 tablespoon lemon juice
2 tablespoons coarsely chopped fresh parsley

1 Place beans in bowl; cover well with cold water. Stand overnight; drain.
2 Cook beans in large saucepan of boiling water; simmer, uncovered, about 30 minutes or until tender; drain well.
3 Meanwhile, coarsely chop goat. Heat oil in large saucepan; cook goat, in batches, until well browned. Remove from pan.
4 Cook onion and garlic in same pan, stirring, until onion softens. Return goat to pan with undrained tomatoes, wine, paste and cinnamon; simmer, covered, 2 hours or until goat is tender, stirring occasionally.
5 Add beans, juice and parsley; season to taste. Stir until heated through.

prep + cook time 2 hours 30 minutes (+ standing) **serves** 6
nutritional count per serving 32.4g total fat (12g saturated fat); 2855kJ (683 cal); 17.8g carbohydrate; 77g protein; 7.6g fibre
tip You will need to order goat from a specialist continental butcher; this casserole is equally delicious made using lamb. Ask the butcher to bone the leg for you.

Braised lamb meatballs in red wine

750g (1½ pounds) minced (ground) lamb
1 cup (70g) stale breadcrumbs
1 cup (80g) coarsely grated kefalograviera cheese
¾ cup finely chopped fresh flat-leaf parsley
2 eggs
2 teaspoons ground cinnamon
1 tablespoon olive oil
1 large brown onion (200g), chopped finely
1 bay leaf
½ cup (125ml) dry red wine
400g (12½ ounces) canned diced tomatoes
1 teaspoon ground allspice

1 Combine lamb, breadcrumbs, cheese, three-quarters of the parsley, eggs and cinnamon in large bowl; season. Roll ¼-cups of mixture into balls.
2 Heat oil in deep frying pan; cook meatballs until browned. Remove from pan.
3 Cook onion and bay leaf in same pan, stirring, until onion softens. Return meatballs to pan with wine; bring to the boil. Reduce heat; simmer, uncovered, until wine has almost evaporated. Stir in undrained tomatoes and allspice. Simmer, covered, about 15 minutes or until meatballs are cooked through. Serve sprinkled with remaining parsley.

prep + cook time 45 minutes **serves** 4
nutritional count per serving 38.9g total fat (15.2g saturated fat); 2588kJ (618 cal); 13.3g carbohydrate; 52.3g protein; 3.6g fibre
serving suggestion Fettuccine.

VEGETARIAN

Eggplant, tomato and chickpea casserole

2 medium eggplants (600g), sliced thickly
2 tablespoons olive oil
150g (4½ ounces) green beans, trimmed, halved
10 spring onions (250g), trimmed
2 cloves garlic, crushed
3 stalks celery (450g), trimmed, sliced thinly
2 x 310g (10 ounces) canned chickpeas (garbanzo beans), rinsed, drained
4 large tomatoes (880g), peeled, chopped finely
¼ cup each finely chopped fresh flat-leaf parsley and oregano
1 tablespoon tomato paste

1 Preheat oven to 180°C/350°F. Preheat grill (broiler).
2 Place eggplant slices on oiled oven tray; brush lightly with half the oil. Place under hot grill until browned both sides.
3 Meanwhile, boil, steam or microwave beans until tender; drain.
4 Heat remaining oil in large flameproof dish; cook onion, stirring, until browned lightly. Stir in eggplant, garlic, celery, chickpeas, tomato and herbs. Cook, covered, in oven 45 minutes or until vegetables are tender. Remove from oven; stir in paste and beans.

prep + cook time 1 hour 20 minutes **serves** 4
nutritional count per serving 12.2g total fat (1.6g saturated fat); 1262kJ (302 cal); 28.1g carbohydrate; 12.9g protein; 14.7g fibre
serving suggestions Warmed crusty bread and yogurt.

Chickpeas with banana chillies

1 cup (200g) dried chickpeas (garbanzo beans)
400g (12½ ounces) canned chopped tomatoes
5 banana chillies (750g), halved lengthways, seeded
1 large red onion (300g), cut into wedges
½ cup coarsely chopped fresh flat-leaf parsley
1 tablespoon rigani
4 bay leaves
2 cloves garlic, sliced thinly
½ cup (125ml) dry white wine
3½ cups (875ml) water
¼ cup (20g) finely grated kefalotyri cheese

1 Place chickpeas in large bowl; cover well with water. Stand overnight.
2 Preheat oven to 160°C/325°F.
3 Drain chickpeas; place in 2.5-litre (10-cup) ovenproof dish. Stir in undrained tomatoes, top with chillies and onion. Sprinkle with herbs and garlic; season with pepper. Add wine and the water. Bake, covered, 1 hour. Uncover, bake further 30 minutes or until chickpeas are tender and liquid is reduced. Season to taste.
4 Serve sprinkled with cheese.

prep + cook time 2 hours 45 minutes (+ standing) **serves** 4
nutritional count per serving 3.2g total fat (1.1g saturated fat); 653kJ (156 cal); 20.5g carbohydrate; 8.8g protein; 21.6g fibre
tip If kefalotyri cheese is unavailable, use parmesan cheese.
serving suggestions Crusty bread and rocket (arugula) salad.

Barbecued vegetables and haloumi with lemon basil dressing

150g (4½ ounces) baby spinach leaves
200g (6½ ounces) char-grilled red capsicum (bell pepper), sliced thickly
250g (8 ounces) grilled artichokes, halved
½ cup (80g) seeded green olives
8 portobello mushrooms (400g)
400g (12½ ounces) haloumi cheese, sliced thickly
lemon basil dressing
2 tablespoons lemon juice
⅓ cup (80ml) olive oil
1 clove garlic, crushed
2 tablespoons finely shredded fresh basil

1 Combine spinach, capsicum, artichokes and olives in large bowl.
2 Cook mushrooms on heated oiled grill plate (or grill or barbecue), loosely covered with foil, about 5 minutes or until browned and tender. Cover to keep warm.
3 Meanwhile, make lemon basil dressing.
4 Cook cheese on same grill plate, in batches, over high heat until browned lightly on both sides.
5 Divide salad among serving dishes, top with mushrooms, cheese and dressing.
lemon basil dressing Place ingredients in screw-top jar; shake well.

prep + cook time 20 minutes **serves** 4
nutritional count per serving 40.8g total fat (14.2g saturated fat); 2169kJ (519 cal); 9.3g carbohydrate; 27.8g protein; 3.9g fibre
tip Portobello is another name for mature swiss brown mushrooms. Large, dark brown mushrooms with full-bodied flavour, these are ideal for barbecuing, and can be stuffed and grilled for a starter or light lunch.

Braised borlotti beans with tomato and garlic

500g (1 pound) fresh borlotti beans, shelled
⅓ cup (80ml) olive oil
1 cup (250ml) water
1 bulb garlic, cut in half horizontally
3 large ripe tomatoes (450g), chopped coarsely
¼ cup fresh oregano leaves
½ cup coarsely chopped fresh basil

1 Preheat oven to 180°C/350°F.
2 Place beans in medium baking dish; drizzle with oil and the water. Add garlic, tomato and oregano; bake, covered, about 1¼ hours or until beans are tender. Stir in basil.

prep + cook time 1 hour 25 minutes **serves** 4
nutritional count per serving 18.4g total fat (2.6g saturated fat); 752kJ (180 cal); 2.3g carbohydrate; 1.2g protein; 1.6g fibre

Eggplant, fetta and capsicum stack with mesclun salad

2 medium red capsicums (bell peppers) (400g)
¼ cup (60ml) olive oil
2 tablespoons lemon juice
1 clove garlic, crushed
1 large eggplant (500g)
1 cup (150g) drained sun-dried tomatoes, chopped coarsely
¼ cup (40g) seeded kalamata olives, chopped coarsely
½ cup loosely packed fresh basil, torn
100g (3 ounces) mesclun
2 tablespoons red wine vinegar
200g (6½ ounces) fetta cheese, cut into 8 slices
1 tablespoon small whole fresh basil leaves, extra

1 Quarter capsicums; discard seeds and membranes. Roast on heated oiled grill plate (or grill or barbecue), skin-side down, until skin blisters and blackens. Cover with plastic or paper for 5 minutes; peel away skin.
2 Meanwhile, combine 2 tablespoons of the oil in small bowl with juice and garlic. Cut eggplant lengthways into eight slices; brush eggplant with a little of the oil mixture. Cook eggplant on same grill plate, brushing occasionally with remaining oil mixture, until just tender.
3 Combine tomato, olives and basil in small bowl. Place mesclun in medium bowl with vinegar and remaining oil; toss gently to combine.
4 Place one slice of the eggplant on each serving plate; top each with two slices of the cheese, two pieces of the capsicum and another slice of eggplant. Top with tomato mixture, sprinkle with extra basil leaves; serve with salad.

prep + cook time 30 minutes **serves** 4
nutritional count per serving 27.8g total fat (9.8g saturated); 1777kJ (425 cal); 23g carbohydrate; 16.4g protein; 10.3g fibre

Char-grilled vegetables with fresh oregano dressing

1 medium red capsicum (bell pepper) (200g)
1 medium yellow capsicum (bell pepper) (200g)
1 large red onion (300g), halved, cut into wedges
1 small kumara (orange sweet potato) (250g), sliced thinly lengthways
2 baby eggplants (120g), sliced thinly lengthways
2 medium zucchini (240g), halved lengthways
340g (11 ounces) bottled artichoke hearts, drained, halved
100g (3 ounces) seeded black olives
1 small radicchio (150g), trimmed, leaves separated

fresh oregano dressing

¼ cup (60ml) olive oil
2 tablespoons red wine vinegar
2 tablespoons lemon juice
2 cloves garlic, crushed
1 tablespoon finely chopped fresh oregano

1 Quarter capsicums, discard seeds and membranes; cut capsicum into thick strips.
2 Make fresh oregano dressing.
3 Cook capsicum, in batches, on heated oiled grill plate (or grill or barbecue) until browned and tender. Remove from grill plate.
4 Cook onion, kumara, eggplant, zucchini and artichokes, in batches, on same grill plate until browned. Remove from grill plate.
5 Place char-grilled vegetables in large bowl with olives and dressing; toss gently to combine. Serve vegetables with radicchio.
fresh oregano dressing Place ingredients in screw-top jar; shake well.

prep + cook time 55 minutes **serves** 4
nutritional count per serving 14.8g total fat (2g saturated fat); 1104kJ (264 cal); 22.8g carbohydrate; 6.4g protein; 7.6g fibre
tip This robust salad can be made ahead with great success: the flavours of the dressing's fresh oregano and lemon will permeate the grilled vegetables and make them even more delicious.

Summer vegetable terrine

2 large red capsicums (bell peppers) (700g)
2 medium yellow capsicums (bell peppers) (400g)
1 large zucchini (300g), sliced thinly lengthways
1 large red onion (300g), sliced thinly
1 tablespoon olive oil
1 teaspoon dried mint leaves
2 medium tomatoes (300g), sliced thinly
300g (9½ ounces) fetta cheese, crumbled coarsely
2 tablespoons each coarsely chopped fresh flat-leaf parsley and dill

1 Preheat oven to 200°C/400°F. Oil 1-litre (4-cup) ovenproof terrine dish or loaf pan; line base with baking paper, extending paper 10cm (4 inches) over long sides.
2 Quarter capsicums; discard seeds and membranes. Roast capsicum, skin-side up, under hot grill or in very hot oven, until skin blisters and blackens. Cover capsicum with plastic or paper for 5 minutes; peel away skin then slice thinly.
3 Meanwhile, place zucchini and onion on separate oiled oven trays. Drizzle with oil, sprinkle with mint; season. Roast, uncovered, about 15 minutes or until tender.
4 Combine cheese and herbs in small bowl; season.
5 Place one-third of the zucchini over base of terrine dish, top with one-third each of the onion, tomato, cheese mixture and capsicum. Repeat layering with remaining ingredients. Cover with baking paper.
6 Bake terrine 20 minutes; cool. Cover terrine with baking paper, weight with another dish filled with heavy cans; refrigerate overnight.

prep + cook time 1 hour (+ cooling & refrigeration)
serves 6 as a light meal
nutritional count per serving 15g total fat (8g saturated fat); 937kJ (224 cal); 9.3g carbohydrate; 12.6g protein; 4.9g fibre
tip To save time, you can use purchased roasted capsicum.
serving suggestions Best served at room temperature. Serve with a mixed green leaf salad.

Slow-cooked potatoes with wine and herbs

1 medium lemon (140g)
600g (1 ¼ pounds) kipfler potatoes, halved lengthways
1 tablespoon olive oil
1 medium brown onion (150g), sliced thinly
12 unpeeled garlic cloves
1 tablespoon rigani
4 bay leaves
½ cup (125ml) dry white wine
1 cup (250ml) chicken stock
⅓ cup (50g) kalamata olives
⅓ cup (65g) fetta cheese, crumbled

1 Preheat oven to 160°C/325°F.
2 Finely grate rind from the lemon. Squeeze lemon; you need ¼ cup juice. Combine potatoes and juice in bowl; season.
3 Heat oil in medium baking dish; cook onion and garlic, stirring, until onion softens. Add potatoes with juice, rigani, rind and bay leaves; stir to coat in onion mixture. Add wine and stock; bring to the boil.
4 Roast potato mixture, uncovered, in oven, stirring occasionally, about 40 minutes or until potatoes are tender.
5 Serve potatoes with olives and fetta.

prep + cook time 55 minutes **serves** 4 as a side
nutritional count per serving 11g total fat (3.6g saturated fat); 970kJ (232 cal); 22.8g carbohydrate; 8g protein; 5.3g fibre

Broad beans and artichokes

300g (9½ ounces) fresh or frozen broad (fava) beans
400g (12½ ounces) canned artichokes, drained, halved
tomato dressing
1 medium tomato (150g), seeded, chopped finely
2 tablespoons finely shredded fresh basil leaves
2 tablespoons olive oil
1 tablespoon white wine vinegar

1 Make tomato dressing.
2 Add shelled broad beans to saucepan of boiling salted water, boil, uncovered, about 2 minutes or until skins wrinkle; drain. Transfer to bowl of iced water, stand 2 minutes; drain. Peel broad beans; discard shell.
3 Place beans in medium bowl with artichokes and dressing; toss gently to combine. Season to taste.
tomato dressing Combine ingredients in small bowl; season to taste.

prep + cook time 20 minutes **serves** 4
nutritional count per serving 9.5g total fat (1.5g saturated fat); 539kJ (129 cal); 4.4g carbohydrate; 6.1g protein; 10.6g fibre
tip You will need about 1.25kg (2½ pounds) fresh broad beans for this recipe.

Braised green beans

4 silver beet (swiss chard) leaves (350g)
1 tablespoon olive oil
1 small onion (80g), sliced thinly
2 cloves garlic, sliced thinly
1 fresh small red chilli, sliced thinly
8 baby potatoes (200g), quartered
300g (9½ ounces) baby green beans, trimmed
400g (12½ ounces) canned chopped tomatoes

1 Wash and dry silver beet; chop leaves and stems finely.
2 Heat oil in medium heavy-based saucepan; cook silver beet stems, onion, garlic and chilli, stirring, about 10 minutes or until stems soften.
3 Add potato and undrained tomatoes; simmer, covered, 15 minutes. Add beans; cook about 5 minutes until potato is tender. Season to taste.
4 Just before serving, add silver beet leaves; cook about 3 minutes or until wilted.

prep + cook time 45 minutes **serves** 6 as a side
nutritional count per serving 3.4g total fat (0.5g saturated fat); 346kJ (83 cal); 9g carbohydrate; 3.7g protein; 4.5g fibre

Celebration

New year cake (vasilopita)

125g (4 ounces) butter, softened
2 teaspoons finely grated orange rind
¾ cup (165g) caster (superfine) sugar
2 eggs, separated
2 cups (300g) self-raising flour
1 cup (250ml) milk
⅓ cup (25g) flaked almonds

1 Preheat oven to 180°C/350°F. Grease 20cm (8-inch) springform tin; line base and side with baking paper.
2 Beat butter, rind, sugar and egg yolks in small bowl with electric mixer until light and fluffy. Transfer mixture to large bowl. Stir in sifted flour and milk, in two batches.
3 Beat egg whites in small bowl with electric mixer until soft peaks form; fold into cake mixture, in two batches. Spread mixture into pan; sprinkle with nuts.
4 Bake cake about 50 minutes. Stand cake in tin 10 minutes before turning top-side up onto wire rack to cool.

prep + cook time 1 hour 20 minutes (+ cooling) **serves** 10
nutritional count per serving 13.6g total fat (7.6g saturated fat); 1268kJ (303cal); 40g carbohydrate; 6g protein; 1.4g fibre
tip Traditionally, a coin would be inserted into the mixture before baking so that the person who found it would have good luck for the coming year. If you want to do this, wrap the coin in foil first (and perhaps warn your guests).
serving suggestion Greek-style yogurt.

Easter cheese pies (flaounes)

2 teaspoons (7g) dry yeast
1 cup (250ml) warm water
1 cup (250ml) warm milk
1 teaspoon salt
2 teaspoons caster (superfine) sugar
5 cups (750g) plain (all-purpose) flour
2 tablespoons olive oil
40g (1½ ounces) butter, melted
1 egg, beaten lightly
¼ cup (35g) sesame seeds

cheese filling
2 cups (250g) coarsely grated kasseri cheese
1⅓ cups (180g) coarsely grated haloumi cheese
1 tablespoon semolina
2 tablespoons finely chopped fresh mint
4 eggs

1 Combine yeast, the water, milk, salt and sugar in small bowl. Cover; stand in warm place about 10 minutes or until frothy.
2 Sift flour into large bowl, stir in yeast mixture, then oil and butter, mix to soft dough. Knead dough on floured surface about 5 minutes or until smooth and elastic. Place dough in large oiled bowl, turn to coat. Cover; stand in warm place about 1 hour or until doubled in size.
3 Meanwhile, preheat oven to 220°C/425°F. Oil four oven trays; line with baking paper.
4 Make cheese filling.
5 Knead dough on floured surface 2 minutes. Working with half the dough at a time, roll dough to 5mm (¼-inch) thick; cut out 10.5cm (4¼-inch) rounds. Drop level tablespoons of filling into centre of each round; brush edge with egg. Shape into a triangle by folding over three sides; pinch edges together, leaving a little filling exposed. Place on trays 3cm (1¼ inches) apart; brush with more egg, sprinkle with seeds.
6 Bake flaounes about 15 minutes or until browned and puffed. Serve warm or cold.
cheese filling Combine ingredients in medium bowl; season.

prep + cook time 1 hour (+ standing) **makes** 32
nutritional count per pastry 6.8g total fat (3.1g saturated fat); 686kJ (164 cal); 18.3g carbohydrate; 7.4g protein; 1g fibre

Easter butter biscuits (koulourakia)

125g (4 ounces) butter, melted
1 teaspoon vanilla extract
2 teaspoons finely grated orange rind
⅔ cup (150g) caster (superfine) sugar
2 eggs
2 tablespoons milk
3 cups (450g) self-raising flour
1 egg yolk, extra
2 tablespoons sesame seeds
¼ cup (35g) slivered almonds

1 Preheat oven to 180°C/350°F. Grease oven trays; line with baking paper.
2 Beat butter, extract, rind and sugar in small bowl with electric mixer until combined. Beat in eggs, one at a time; do not over-beat. Transfer mixture to large bowl; stir in milk and sifted flour, in two batches. Turn dough onto floured surface; knead lightly until smooth.
3 Divide dough into 10 balls, divide each ball into five balls. Roll each ball into 15cm (6-inch) sausage-shaped lengths, then cut into 10cm (4-inch) lengths. Shape lengths into scrolls, twists and figure eights; place about 2.5cm (1 inch) apart on trays. Brush with extra egg yolk, sprinkle with seeds and nuts.
4 Bake biscuits about 15 minutes; cool on trays.

prep + cook time 1 hour **makes** 50
nutritional count per biscuit 3g total fat (1.5g saturated fat); 300kJ (72 cal); 9.6g carbohydrate; 1.6g protein; 0.5g fibre

Easter bread (tsoureki)

6 teaspoons (21g) dry yeast
½ cup (125ml) warm water
1 cup (250ml) warm milk
1 teaspoon salt
1 teaspoon caster (superfine) sugar
155g (5 ounces) butter, softened
2 teaspoons finely grated lemon rind
1 cup (220g) caster (superfine) sugar, extra
4 eggs
6 cups (900g) plain (all-purpose) flour
2 teaspoons ground cinnamon
1 egg yolk, extra
¼ cup (20g) flaked almonds

1 Combine yeast, the water, half the milk, salt and sugar in small bowl. Cover; stand in warm place about 10 minutes or until frothy.
2 Beat butter, rind and extra sugar in small bowl with electric mixer until light and fluffy. Beat in eggs, one at a time, then remaining cooled milk (mixture will curdle at this stage, but will come together later).
3 Sift flour and cinnamon into large bowl, stir in yeast and butter mixtures; mix to a soft dough. Knead dough on floured surface about 5 minutes or until smooth and elastic. Place dough in large greased bowl. Cover; stand in warm place about 1 hour or until doubled in size.
4 Meanwhile, preheat oven to 220°C/425°F. Grease two oven trays; line with baking paper.
5 Knead dough on floured surface 2 minutes. Divide dough in half, divide each half into thirds. Roll each third into sausage-shaped lengths of about 45cm (18 inches). Plait three lengths together, shape into a ring. Repeat with remaining lengths. Place on trays; cover, stand in warm place about 30 minutes or until doubled in size.
6 Brush bread with extra egg yolk, sprinkle with nuts. Bake 20 minutes, reduce oven to 180°C/350°F; bake further 20 minutes or until browned. Cool on tray 5 minutes. Serve warm or cold.

prep + cook time 1 hour 30 minutes (+ standing) **serves** 16
nutritional count per serving 10.9g total fat (5.9g saturated fat); 1496kJ (357 cal); 56.3g carbohydrate; 8.8g protein; 2.5g fibre
tips A few red-dyed, hard-boiled eggs can also be positioned at even intervals when plaiting the dough. You can decorate the bread with sesame seeds or slivered almonds.

Deep-fried sweet pastries (thiples)

2 cups (300g) self-raising flour
2 teaspoons caster (superfine) sugar
½ teaspoon salt
2 eggs
1 tablespoon olive oil
¼ cup (60ml) water
vegetable oil, for deep-frying
1 cup (350g) honey, warmed
1 teaspoon ground cinnamon
½ cup (50g) roasted walnuts, chopped finely

1 Sift flour, sugar and salt into large bowl; stir in combined eggs, olive oil and the water. Turn dough onto floured surface, knead until smooth. Enclose in plastic wrap; refrigerate 30 minutes.
2 Divide dough evenly into four pieces. Roll each piece as thinly as possible into about 15cm x 45cm (6-inch x18-inch) rectangle. Cut into 5cm x 15cm (2-inch x 6-inch) strips.
3 Shape strips into bows or roll into spirals or twist or cut a slit in the strip of dough and pull through.
4 Heat vegetable oil in large saucepan or wok; deep-fry pastries, in batches, turning often, until browned lightly. Drain on absorbent paper.
5 Transfer pastries to serving plate. Drizzle with honey; sprinkle with combined cinnamon and walnuts.

prep + cook time 1 hour (+ refrigeration) **makes** 36
nutritional count per pastry 2.6g total fat (0.3g saturated fat); 355kJ (85 cal); 14.3g carbohydrate; 1.5g protein; 0.4g fibre

Walnut cake

9 eggs, separated
¾ cup (165g) caster (superfine) sugar
⅓ cup (80ml) brandy
¾ cup (180ml) orange juice
1 teaspoon vanilla extract
1½ cups (180g) finely chopped walnuts
1½ cups (150g) packaged breadcrumbs
1 teaspoon ground cinnamon
¼ teaspoon each ground cloves and allspice
1 teaspoon bicarbonate of soda (baking soda)

syrup
1 cup (220g) caster (superfine) sugar
2 cups (500ml) water
1 cinnamon stick
1 strip orange rind

1 Preheat oven to 200°C/400°F. Grease deep 20cm x 30cm (8-inch x 12-inch) ovenproof dish; line with baking paper, extending paper 5cm (2 inches) over short sides.
2 Beat egg yolks and ½ cup (110g) of the sugar in small bowl with electric mixer until light and fluffy. Transfer mixture to large bowl; stir in brandy, juice and extract, then nuts, breadcrumbs and sifted spices and soda.
3 Beat egg whites in large bowl with electric mixer until soft peaks form. Gradually add remaining sugar, beating until sugar dissolves between additions; fold into walnut mixture, in two batches. Pour mixture into dish.
4 Bake cake about 40 minutes. Cool cake in dish.
5 Meanwhile, make syrup.
6 Pour hot syrup over cake.
syrup Stir ingredients in small saucepan over heat until sugar dissolves. Bring to the boil; boil, uncovered, without stirring, 10 minutes.

prep + cook time 1 hour 15 minutes (+ cooling) **makes** 18
nutritional count per piece 9.5g total fat (1.3g saturated fat); 946kJ (226 cal); 28g carbohydrate; 5.8g protein; 1.1g fibre

Halva

2 cups (440g) caster (superfine) sugar
1 litre (4 cups) water
2 cloves
1 cinnamon stick
220g (7 ounces) butter, chopped coarsely
2 cups (320g) semolina
½ cup (80g) coarsely chopped blanched almonds
2 teaspoons finely grated orange rind
½ cup (80g) coarsely chopped raisins
¼ cup (40g) blanched whole almonds, roasted, extra
1 teaspoon ground cinnamon

1 Grease 20cm x 30cm (8-inch x 12-inch) slice pan or ovenproof dish; line base with baking paper, extending paper 5cm (2 inches) over short sides.
2 Stir sugar, the water, cloves and cinnamon stick in medium saucepan over heat until sugar dissolves. Bring to the boil; boil, uncovered, without stirring, 5 minutes. Cool 5 minutes.
3 Meanwhile, heat butter in large saucepan until foaming. Add semolina and chopped nuts; cook, stirring, about 8 minutes or until lightly browned. Remove from heat. Carefully strain sugar syrup into semolina mixture (mixture will bubble up).
4 Return pan to heat, add rind and raisins; cook, stirring, about 1 minute or until thick and starting to come away from the side of the pan.
5 Spread semolina mixture into pan; top with extra nuts, cool. Sprinkle with ground cinnamon before cutting.

prep + cook time 30 minutes (+ standing) **serves** 20
nutritional count per serving 12.4g total fat (6g saturated fat); 1097kJ (262 cal); 36g carbohydrate; 3g protein; 1.3g fibre

Moist carrot and apple cake

2 cups (300g) self-raising flour
1 teaspoon bicarbonate of soda (baking soda)
1 cup (220g) caster (superfine) sugar
4 cups (960g) coarsely grated carrot
2 cups (340g) coarsely grated apple
1 tablespoon finely grated orange rind
¼ cup (60ml) orange juice
¾ cup (180ml) olive oil
⅓ cup (80ml) brandy
1 cup (150g) roasted pine nuts
2 teaspoons icing (confectioners') sugar

1 Preheat oven to 180°C/350°F. Grease 25cm (10-inch) springform tin; line base and side with baking paper.
2 Sift flour and soda into large bowl; stir in caster sugar, carrot, apple and rind. Stir in juice, oil, brandy and pine nuts. Pour mixture into pan.
3 Bake cake about 1 hour. Stand cake 10 minutes before removing from springform tin. Serve dusted with sifted icing sugar.

prep + cook time 1 hour 20 minutes (+ standing) **serves** 12
nutritional count per serving 22.8g total fat (2.8g saturated fat); 1720kJ (410 cal); 44.5g carbohydrate; 5g protein; 5.3g fibre

Almond fingers (thaktila)

3 cups (450g) plain (all-purpose) flour
½ cup (125ml) olive oil
1 cup (250ml) water
2 egg yolks
1½ cups (240g) roasted blanched almonds, chopped finely
1½ teaspoons ground cinnamon
2 tablespoons caster (superfine) sugar
1 egg white, beaten lightly
vegetable oil, for deep-frying

honey syrup
1 cup (220g) caster (superfine) sugar
1 cup (360g) honey
2 cups (500ml) water
1 cinnamon stick
1 strip lemon rind
1 tablespoon lemon juice
2 cloves

1 Sift flour into large bowl, stir in olive oil, the water and egg yolks. Knead dough on floured surface until smooth. Enclose in plastic wrap; refrigerate 30 minutes.
2 Meanwhile, make honey syrup.
3 Combine nuts, cinnamon and sugar in small bowl.
4 Divide dough in half. Roll as thinly as possible (about 1.5mm thick); cut into 10cm (4-inch) squares. Place 2 teaspoons of nut mixture along the centre of each square. Brush edges with a little egg white; roll into cigar shape; use a fork to press ends to seal. Repeat with remaining dough and nut mixture.
5 Heat vegetable oil in large saucepan or wok; deep-fry pastries, three or four at a time, turning frequently, until browned lightly. Drain briefly on absorbent paper then submerge in warm honey syrup; drain on wire rack over a tray. Serve warm or cooled.
honey syrup Stir ingredients in medium saucepan over heat until sugar dissolves. Bring to the boil. Reduce heat; simmer, uncovered, without stirring, about 15 minutes or until syrup is thick.

prep + cook time 1 hour 15 minutes (+ refrigeration) **makes** 35
nutritional count per pastry 9.3g total fat (1.1g saturated fat); 811kJ (194 cal); 25.4g carbohydrate; 3.1g protein; 1.2g fibre

Sweets

Cherry spoon sweet

425g (13½ ounces) canned seedless black cherries in syrup
1 cup (220g) caster (superfine) sugar
1 vanilla bean, split lengthways
2 x 5cm (2-inch) strips lemon rind
1 teaspoon lemon juice

1 Drain cherries over small saucepan; reserve cherries.
2 Add sugar, vanilla bean, rind and juice to pan; stir over heat until sugar dissolves.
3 Add reserved cherries, bring to the boil; boil, uncovered, about 7 minutes or until mixture thickens and will coat the back of a metal spoon. Cool to room temperature.

prep + cook time 15 minutes (+ cooling) **serves** 6
nutritional count per serving 0.1g total fat (0g saturated fat); 800kJ (191 cal); 48.7g carbohydrate; 0.6g protein; 0.7g fibre
serving suggestion This is traditionally served with a glass of cold water when guests arrive.

Orange spoon sweet

3 medium oranges (720g)
2 cups (440g) caster (superfine) sugar
1 1/4 cups (310ml) water
1 teaspoon lemon juice

1 Using a vegetable peeler, remove and discard the rind from oranges. Trim the ends from the oranges to expose the orange flesh. Cut each orange into 8 wedges; cut the white pith away from the flesh. Reserve flesh for another use. Cut strips of pith in half diagonally.
2 Place pith in medium saucepan with enough cold water to cover completely. Bring to the boil; boil, uncovered, 5 minutes. Drain, rinse pith under cold water. Repeat process two more times. Dry pith on absorbent paper for 30 minutes.
3 Stir sugar and the water in small saucepan over heat until sugar dissolves. Add pith; bring to the boil. Boil, uncovered, about 10 minutes or until mixture thickens enough to coat the back of a metal spoon. Stir in juice. Cool to room temperature.

prep + cook time 1 hour (+ standing & cooling) **serves** 12
nutritional count per serving 0g total fat (0g saturated fat); 588kJ (140 cal); 36.7g carbohydrate; 0g protein; 0.2g fibre
serving suggestion This is traditionally served with a glass of cold water when guests arrive.

Honey walnut biscuits

1 cup (250ml) vegetable oil
½ cup (110g) caster (superfine) sugar
½ cup (125ml) orange juice
2 tablespoons brandy
1 egg
4 cups (600g) self-raising flour
1 cup (160g) fine semolina
1 teaspoon ground cinnamon
1 cup (100g) walnut pieces, chopped finely
spiced syrup
1 cup (220g) caster (superfine) sugar
½ cup (175g) honey
½ cup (125ml) water
2 tablespoons lemon juice
1 cinnamon stick
6 cloves

1 Preheat oven to 160°C/325°F. Grease oven trays; line with baking paper.
2 Combine oil, sugar, juice, brandy and egg in large bowl. Stir in sifted flour, semolina and half the cinnamon.
3 Roll level tablespoons of mixture into 6cm (2½-inch) oval shapes. Place on trays, about 4cm (1½ inches) apart.
4 Bake biscuits about 25 minutes. Cool on trays.
5 Meanwhile, make spiced syrup.
6 Dip biscuits, in batches, into hot syrup for about 30 seconds or until well coated; transfer to wire rack. Sprinkle biscuits with combined walnuts and remaining cinnamon. Cool.
spiced syrup Stir ingredients in small saucepan over heat until sugar dissolves; bring to the boil. Reduce heat; simmer, uncovered, about 7 minutes or until thickened slightly. Strain into heatproof bowl.

prep + cook time 55 minutes (+ cooling) **makes** 48
nutritional count per biscuit 15.8g total fat (1.8g saturated fat); 1545kJ (370cal); 51.8g carbohydrate; 5.2g protein; 1.8g fibre

Rice pudding with cinnamon and vanilla bean

3 cups (750ml) milk
¼ cup (55g) caster (superfine) sugar
2 x 5cm (2-inch) strips lemon rind
1 vanilla bean, split lengthways
1 cinnamon stick
⅓ cup (65g) white medium-grain rice
3 egg yolks
⅓ cup (35g) walnuts, roasted, chopped coarsely
¼ teaspoon ground cinnamon

1 Combine milk, sugar and rind in medium saucepan; bring to the boil, stirring occasionally. Add vanilla bean and cinnamon stick, gradually stir in rice; cook, covered tightly, over low heat, stirring occasionally, about 40 minutes or until rice is tender. Discard rind, cinnamon stick and vanilla bean.

2 Combine 1 tablespoon of the hot milk mixture with egg yolks in small heatproof jug. Pour egg yolk mixture into rice, stirring over low heat, until mixture thickens.

3 Serve pudding sprinkled with nuts and ground cinnamon.

prep + cook time 55 minutes **serves** 4
nutritional count per serving 11.6g total fat (5.6g saturated fat); 1282kJ (306 cal); 42g carbohydrate; 9.8g protein; 0.4g fibre
tip This dish can be served warm or cooled.

Baklava

1 ½ cups (200g) shelled unsalted pistachio nuts
2 cups (200g) walnut pieces
¼ cup (55g) caster (superfine) sugar
2 tablespoons fine semolina
1 teaspoon ground cinnamon
pinch ground cloves
375g (12 ounces) fillo pastry
310g (10 ounces) butter, melted
30 whole cloves

syrup
1 cup (220g) caster (superfine) sugar
1 cup (250ml) water
¼ cup (90g) honey
1 tablespoon lemon juice
1 cinnamon stick

1 Preheat oven to 200°C/400°F. Grease 20cm x 30cm (8-inch x 12-inch) lamington pan.
2 Process nuts, sugar, semolina, cinnamon and ground cloves until chopped finely; transfer to medium bowl.
3 Brush 1 sheet of pastry with a little of the butter; top with 7 more sheets, brushing each well with butter. Fold pastry in half, place into pan. Sprinkle pastry with thin even layer of the nut mixture. Layer another 2 sheets of pastry, brushing each well with more butter. Fold pastry in half, place in pan; top with another layer of nut mixture. Repeat layering process until all nut mixture has been used. Repeat layering and buttering with any remaining pastry sheets; brush the final layer with butter. Score the top lightly in diamond pattern; press one whole clove into centre of each piece.
4 Bake baklava about 50 minutes.
5 Meanwhile, make syrup.
6 Pour syrup over hot baklava. Cool before cutting.
syrup Stir ingredients in small saucepan over heat until sugar dissolves; bring to the boil. Reduce heat; simmer, uncovered, about 10 minutes or until thickened slightly. Discard cinnamon; cool syrup.

prep + cook time 1 hour 20 minutes (+ cooling) **makes** 30
nutritional count per piece 16.4g total fat (6.1g saturated fat); 1010kJ (240 cal); 21g carbohydrate; 3.6g protein; 1.4g fibre

Almond and walnut pastries (kataifi)

1 cup (160g) almond kernels, chopped finely
½ cup (50g) walnut pieces, chopped finely
½ cup (35g) stale breadcrumbs
2 teaspoons caster (superfine) sugar
1 teaspoon ground cinnamon
1 egg
375g (12 ounce) kataifi pastry
250g (8 ounces) unsalted butter, melted

lemon syrup
2 cups (440g) caster (superfine) sugar
1 cup (250ml) water
¼ cup (90g) honey
4 x 5cm (2-inch) strips lemon rind
2 tablespoons lemon juice

1 Preheat oven to 200°C/400°F. Grease 20cm x 30cm (8-inch x 12-inch) lamington pan.
2 Combine nuts, breadcrumbs, sugar, cinnamon and egg in medium bowl.
3 Lightly pull the pastry apart. Spread ½ cup of pastry into 5cm x 20cm (2-inch x 8-inch) rectangular shape; brush with some of the butter. Place 1 level tablespoon of the nut mixture along one short side of the pastry; roll up tightly, place in pan. Repeat with remaining pastry, butter and nut mixture.
4 Bake pastries about 35 minutes.
5 Meanwhile, make lemon syrup.
6 Pour hot syrup over hot pastries in pan. Cool.
lemon syrup Stir ingredients in small saucepan over heat until sugar dissolves; bring to the boil. Reduce heat; simmer, uncovered, 10 minutes or until thickened slightly. Discard rind.

prep + cook time 55 minutes (+ cooling) **makes** 18
nutritional count per piece 19.1g total fat (8.1g saturated fat); 1500kJ (358 cal); 43.6g carbohydrate; 4.9g protein; 1.6g fibre
tip Kataifi is finely shredded fillo pastry available from Middle Eastern grocery stores. During preparation, keep the pastry covered with baking paper then a damp tea-towel to prevent the pastry drying out.

Galaktoboureko

1.25 litres (5 cups) milk
1¾ cups (385g) caster (superfine) sugar
1 vanilla bean, split lengthways
1 cup (160g) fine semolina
20g (¾ ounce) butter
4 eggs
16 sheets fillo pastry
150g (5 ounces) butter, melted
1 tablespoon icing (confectioners') sugar
¼ teaspoon ground cinnamon

lemon syrup
1 cup (220g) caster (superfine) sugar
¾ cup (180ml) water
2 x 5cm (2 inch) strips lemon rind
2 teaspoons lemon juice

1 Stir milk, sugar and vanilla bean in large saucepan over heat until sugar dissolves; bring to the boil. Gradually whisk semolina into milk mixture; whisk over medium heat about 5 minutes or until thickened.
2 Remove pan from heat; discard vanilla bean. Stir in butter. Transfer custard to large heatproof bowl; cover surface of custard with plastic wrap. Cool 1 hour. Stir in eggs.
3 Preheat oven to 160°C/325°F. Grease deep 25cm x 32cm (10-inch x 13-inch) baking dish.
4 Cut pastry sheets to the same size as dish; discard excess pastry. Brush 1 sheet of pastry with some of the butter; top with 7 more pastry sheets, brushing each with butter. Place in base of dish; spread custard into dish. Repeat with remaining pastry and butter; place on top of custard.
5 Bake galaktoboureko about 55 minutes or until custard is set.
6 Meanwhile, make lemon syrup.
7 Pour hot syrup over hot galaktoboureko; cool. Serve dusted with combined sifted icing sugar and cinnamon.
lemon syrup Stir ingredients in small saucepan over heat until sugar dissolves; bring to the boil. Reduce heat; simmer, uncovered, 10 minutes or until thickened slightly. Discard rind.

prep + cook time 1 hour 40 minutes (+ cooling) **makes** 21
nutritional count per piece 9.8g total fat (5.9g saturated fat); 1182kJ (282 cal); 44.9g carbohydrate; 5.2g protein; 0.5g fibre

Loukoumades

1 cup (250ml) warm water
1 ½ teaspoons (5g) dry yeast
1 teaspoon caster (superfine) sugar
½ teaspoon salt
1 ½ cups (225g) plain (all-purpose) flour
vegetable oil, for deep-frying
1 teaspoon ground cinnamon

honey citrus syrup
1 cup (360g) honey
½ cup (110g) caster (superfine) sugar
½ cup (125ml) water
2 x 5cm (2-inch) strips lemon rind
2 x 5cm (2-inch) strips orange rind

1 Whisk the water, yeast, sugar and salt together in small bowl until yeast is dissolved.
2 Sift flour into large bowl; gradually stir in yeast mixture until smooth. Cover; stand in warm place about 45 minutes or until mixture has doubled in size.
3 Meanwhile, make honey citrus syrup.
4 Heat oil in large saucepan or wok; deep-fry rounded teaspoons of batter, in batches, until browned lightly and cooked through. Drain on absorbent paper.
5 Drizzle hot loukoumades with syrup, sprinkle with cinnamon. Serve loukoumades warm.
honey citrus syrup Stir ingredients in small saucepan over heat until sugar dissolves; bring to the boil. Reduce heat; simmer, 10 minutes or until thickened slightly. Cool.

prep + cook time 35 minutes (+ standing) **makes** 36
nutritional count per piece 1.7g total fat (0.2g saturated fat); 335kJ (80 cal); 16g carbohydrate; 0.7g protein; 0.3g fibre
tip We used Attiki honey in this recipe.

Apricot jam tart

2¼ cups (335g) plain (all-purpose) flour
½ cup (80g) icing (confectioners') sugar
185g (6 ounces) cold butter, chopped
2 egg yolks
2 tablespoons iced water, approximately
⅔ cup (220g) apricot jam, warmed, sieved
1 tablespoon flaked almonds

apricot filling

2 cups (300g) coarsely chopped dried apricots
⅓ cup (50g) raisins
½ cup (125ml) water
¼ cup (55g) caster (superfine) sugar
2 tablespoons brandy
1 tablespoon finely grated lemon rind

1 Process flour, sugar and butter until crumbly. With motor operating, add egg yolks and enough iced water to make ingredients cling together. Turn dough onto floured surface, knead gently until smooth. Shape dough into disc, enclose in plastic wrap; refrigerate 30 minutes.

2 Preheat oven to 160°C/325°F. Grease 11cm x 34cm (4½-inch x 13½-inch) loose-based flan tin.

3 Meanwhile, make apricot filling.

4 Reserve one quarter of the dough. Roll remaining dough between sheets of baking paper until large enough to line tin. Ease dough into tin, press into sides; trim edges, reserve excess dough. Spread apricot filling into pastry case; spread with jam.

5 Roll reserved dough between sheets of baking paper until 5mm (¼-inch) thick; using crinkle-cut pastry cutter, cut 1cm (½-inch) strips from dough. Decorate tart in lattice pattern using pastry strips; sprinkle with nuts. Bake about 50 minutes.

apricot filling Cook ingredients, stirring, in medium saucepan, over medium heat about 10 minutes or until apricots soften. Cool 10 minutes. Blend or process apricot mixture until almost smooth.

prep + cook time 1 hour 40 minutes (+ refrigeration) **serves** 10
nutritional count per serving 16.7g total fat (10.1g saturated fat); 1908kJ (455 cal); 70g carbohydrate; 5.9g protein; 4.4g fibre
serving suggestion Pouring cream.

Coconut syrup cake

125g (4 ounces) butter, softened
1 cup (220g) caster (superfine) sugar
4 eggs
2 cups (160g) desiccated coconut
1 cup (150g) self-raising flour
2 tablespoons desiccated coconut, extra
lemon syrup
1 cup (220g) caster (superfine) sugar
1 cup (250ml) water
4 x 5cm (2-inch) strips lemon rind

1 Preheat oven to 160°C/325°F. Grease deep 20cm (8-inch) round cake pan; line base and side with baking paper.
2 Beat butter and sugar in small bowl with electric mixer until light and fluffy. Beat in eggs one at a time. Transfer mixture to large bowl; stir in coconut and sifted flour. Spread mixture into pan; sprinkle with extra coconut.
3 Bake cake about 50 minutes.
4 Meanwhile, make lemon syrup.
5 Pour hot lemon syrup over hot cake in pan. Cool.
lemon syrup Stir ingredients in small saucepan over heat until sugar dissolves; bring to the boil. Reduce heat; simmer, uncovered, without stirring, 5 minutes. Strain.

prep + cook time 1 hour 10 minutes (+ cooling) **serves** 12
nutritional count per serving 19.5g total fat (13.5g saturated fat); 1556kJ (371 cal); 46.8g carbohydrate; 4.5g protein; 2.7g fibre

Chocolate log cake

4 eggs, separated
½ cup (110g) caster (superfine) sugar
2 teaspoons finely grated lemon rind
⅔ cup (100g) plain (all-purpose) flour
1 tablespoon caster (superfine) sugar, extra
1 tablespoon icing (confectioners') sugar

chocolate filling
155g (5 ounces) unsalted butter, softened
⅔ cup (110g) icing (confectioners') sugar
3 teaspoons dark rum
250g dark eating (semi-sweet) chocolate, melted

1 Preheat oven to 160°C/325°F. Grease 25cm x 30cm (10-inch x 12-inch) swiss roll pan; line base with baking paper, extending paper 5cm (2 inches) over long sides.
2 Beat egg yolks, 2 tablespoons of the caster sugar and rind in small bowl with electric mixer until thick and creamy; transfer to large bowl.
3 Beat egg whites with remaining caster sugar in small bowl with electric mixer until soft peaks form. Fold sifted flour into egg yolk mixture. Fold in egg white mixture, in two batches. Spread mixture into pan.
4 Bake cake about 12 minutes.
5 Meanwhile, place a piece of baking paper cut the same size as pan on bench; sprinkle paper evenly with extra caster sugar. Turn cake onto sugared paper, peel away lining paper. Working rapidly, use serrated knife to trim all sides of cake. Using paper as a guide, gently roll cake loosely from short side. Cool.
6 Make chocolate filling.
7 Unroll cake; spread evenly with 1 cup of the chocolate filling. Re-roll cake, place on plate; spread log all over with remaining chocolate filling. Refrigerate 30 minutes. Serve dusted with sifted icing sugar.
chocolate filling Beat butter, sugar and rum in small bowl with electric mixer until light and fluffy. Beat in cooled chocolate.

prep + cook time 1 hour (+ cooling & refrigeration) **serves** 10
nutritional count per serving 21.6g total fat (13g saturated fat); 1672kJ (400 cal); 47.9g carbohydrate; 5g protein; 0.7g fibre

Milopita

3 medium apples (450g), peeled, cored, quartered
¼ cup (60ml) lemon juice
60g (2 ounces) butter
¼ cup (55g) firmly packed light brown sugar
1 teaspoon ground cinnamon
125g (4 ounces) butter, softened, extra
1 cup (220g) caster (superfine) sugar
1 tablespoon finely grated lemon rind
1 teaspoon vanilla extract
2 eggs, separated
1 cup (150g) self-raising flour
¼ cup (60ml) milk
1 tablespoon icing (confectioners') sugar
brandy yogurt
1½ tablespoons brandy
3 teaspoons light brown sugar
1 cup (280g) greek-style yogurt

1 Preheat oven to 160°C/325°F. Grease 24cm (9½-inch) fluted pie dish.
2 Slice apple thinly; combine in medium bowl with juice. Stir butter, brown sugar and cinnamon in small saucepan over heat until sugar dissolves.
3 Beat extra butter, caster sugar, rind, extract and egg yolks in small bowl with electric mixer until light and fluffy. Stir in sifted flour and milk, in two batches.
4 Beat egg whites in small bowl with electric mixer until soft peaks form; fold into cake mixture, in two batches. Spread mixture into dish.
5 Drain apples; discard juice, return apples to bowl. Stir warm brown sugar mixture into apples. Arrange apple slices over batter in dish; drizzle with brown sugar mixture. Bake about 45 minutes.
6 Meanwhile, make brandy yogurt.
7 Dust milopita with sifted icing sugar; serve warm with brandy yogurt.
brandy yogurt Stir brandy and sugar in small bowl until sugar dissolves; stir in yogurt.

prep + cook time 1 hour 30 minutes **serves** 8
nutritional count per serving 22.5g total fat (14.2g saturated fat); 1962kJ (470 cal); 61.1g carbohydrate; 6.2g protein; 1.8g fibre

Pistachio honey cake

¾ cup (270g) honey
⅔ cup (150g) caster (superfine) sugar
1 tablespoon brandy
1 tablespoon lemon juice
½ cup (125ml) olive oil
2 eggs
155g (5 ounces) ricotta cheese
2 cups (300g) self-raising flour
½ teaspoon each of ground cinnamon, nutmeg and clove
¼ cup (35g) shelled unsalted pistachio nuts
1 tablespoon honey, extra

1 Stir honey, sugar, brandy and juice in small saucepan over heat until sugar dissolves; bring to the boil. Reduce heat, simmer, uncovered, 2 minutes. Cool 20 minutes.
2 Meanwhile, preheat oven to 150°C/300°F. Grease 14cm x 21cm (5½-inch x 8½-inch) loaf pan; line base and two long sides with baking paper.
3 Combine oil, eggs and cheese in large bowl; stir in sifted dry ingredients and cooled honey mixture. Spread mixture into pan; sprinkle with nuts.
4 Bake cake about 1 hour. Turn cake, top-side up, onto wire rack. Drizzle with extra honey; cool before cutting.

prep + cook time 1 hour 30 minutes (+ cooling) **serves** 10
nutritional count per serving 15.6g total fat (3.2g saturated fat); 1723kJ (412 cal); 62g carbohydrate; 6.6g protein; 1.6g fibre

Cheesecake with brandied muscatels

125g (4 ounces) sponge finger biscuits
50g (1½ ounces) unsalted butter, melted
500g (1 pound) unsalted fresh myzithra cheese
½ cup (80g) icing (confectioners') sugar
1 tablespoon finely grated lemon rind
1 tablespoon cornflour (cornstarch)
4 eggs
½ cup (125ml) thickened (heavy) cream
2 tablespoons flaked almonds, chopped coarsely
brandied muscatels
¾ cup (165g) firmly packed light brown sugar
¼ cup (60ml) water
¼ cup (60ml) brandy
1 tablespoon honey
12 small clusters muscatels

1 Preheat oven to 140°C/280°F. Grease 20cm (8-inch) round springform tin; line base and side with baking paper.
2 Process biscuits until fine. Add butter, process until combined. Press mixture firmly over base of tin. Refrigerate 30 minutes.
3 Meanwhile, beat cheese, sifted icing sugar, rind and cornflour in small bowl with electric mixer until smooth. Beat in eggs, one at a time; beat in cream, in two batches. Pour mixture into tin; sprinkle with nuts.
4 Bake cheesecake about 1 hour 10 minutes. Turn oven off; leave to cool completely in oven with door ajar. Cover; refrigerate 1 hour.
5 Meanwhile, make brandied muscatels.
6 Serve cheesecake topped with muscatels and drizzled with syrup.
brandied muscatels Stir sugar, the water, brandy and honey in small saucepan over heat until sugar dissolves; bring to the boil. Reduce heat; simmer, uncovered, without stirring, about 5 minutes or until thickened slightly. Add muscatels; cool.

prep + cook time 1 hour 40 minutes (+ cooling & refrigeration) **serves** 12
nutritional count per serving 29.4g total fat (17.6g saturated fat); 1775kJ (424 cal); 34.5g carbohydrate; 5.1g protein; 0.5g fibre
tip Myzithra cheese is the traditional Greek cheese used in this cheesecake; you could use mascarpone as a substitute in this recipe.

Fried custard tarts

2 cups (500ml) water
½ cup (80g) fine semolina
½ cup (110g) caster (superfine) sugar
1 ½ tablespoons rosewater
¼ teaspoon powdered mastic
3 sheets shortcrust pastry
1 egg, beaten lightly
vegetable oil, for deep-frying
⅓ cup (55g) icing (confectioners') sugar

1 Place the water in small saucepan; bring to gentle simmer. Gradually stir in semolina; add sugar, rosewater and mastic. Cook, stirring, over low heat, about 5 minutes or until thickened. Transfer custard to small heatproof bowl; cover surface of custard with plastic wrap. Cool 1 hour.
2 Cut each pastry sheet in half, then cut each half into three rectangles. Roll one rectangle on floured surface until 12cm (5-inch) square. Place 1 level tablespoon of custard in centre of pastry; brush edges with egg. Fold two opposite edges of pastry over filling to enclose; brush the other two opposite edges with egg and fold to almost meet in the centre. Repeat with remaining pastry and custard.
3 Heat oil in large saucepan or wok; deep-fry pastries, in batches, until browned lightly and crisp. Drain on absorbent paper.
4 Serve immediately, dusted with sifted icing sugar.

prep + cook time 45 minutes (+ cooling) **makes** 18
nutritional count per pastry 11.3g total fat (3.6g saturated fat); 863kJ (206 cal); 24.4g carbohydrate; 2.4g protein; 0.4g fibre
tip Mastic is a natural resin from the mastic tree which grows on the Greek island of Chios. It is used in a variety of baked goods for its licorice-like flavour, and is available from shops that stock Greek and Middle Eastern food.

Yogurt cake

125g (4 ounces) butter, softened
1 cup (220g) caster (superfine) sugar
3 eggs, separated
2 cups (300g) self-raising flour
½ teaspoon bicarbonate of soda (baking soda)
¼ cup (40g) finely chopped blanched almonds
1 cup (280g) yogurt

1 Preheat oven to 180°C/350°F. Grease 20cm x 30cm (8-inch x 12-inch) lamington pan; line base and sides with baking paper.
2 Beat butter and sugar in small bowl with electric mixer until light and fluffy. Beat in egg yolks.
3 Transfer mixture to large bowl; stir in sifted flour and soda, in two batches. Stir in nuts and yogurt.
4 Beat egg whites in clean small bowl with electric mixer until soft peaks form. Fold egg whites into yogurt mixture, in two batches. Spread mixture into pan.
5 Bake cake about 35 minutes. Turn cake onto wire rack to cool.

prep + cook time 1 hour (+ cooling) **serves** 12
nutritional count per serving 12.8g total fat (6.7g saturated fat); 1216kJ (291 cal); 37.3g carbohydrate; 5.9g protein; 1.2g fibre
serving suggestion Dusted icing sugar.

Almond biscuits

3 cups (360g) ground almonds
1 cup (220g) caster (superfine) sugar
3 drops almond essence
3 egg whites, beaten lightly
1 cup (80g) flaked almonds

1 Preheat oven to 180°C/350°F.
2 Combine ground almonds, sugar and essence in large bowl. Add egg whites; stir until mixture forms a firm paste
3 Roll level tablespoons of mixture in flaked almonds; roll into 8cm (3¼-inch) logs. Press on remaining almonds. Shape logs to form crescents; place on baking-paper-lined oven trays.
4 Bake biscuits about 15 minutes or until browned lightly; cool on trays.

prep + cook time 45 minutes (+ cooling) **makes** 25
nutritional count per biscuit 9g total fat (0.6g saturated fat); 568kJ (136 cal); 9.5g carbohydrate; 3.7g protein; 1.4g fibre

Spiced plums with yogurt

2 x 825g (1¾ pounds) canned whole plums
2 cinnamon sticks
6 cardamom pods
1 cup (280g) yogurt

1 Drain juice from plums into medium saucepan. Add cinnamon and cardamom; bring to the boil. Reduce heat; simmer, uncovered, 3 minutes.
2 Remove pan from heat. Add plums; cover pan, stand 10 minutes.
3 Serve warm plums with yogurt; drizzle with juice mixture.

prep + cook time 15 minutes (+ standing) **serves** 6
nutritional count per serving 3.4g total fat (2.1g saturated fat); 543kJ (130 cal); 21.5g carbohydrate; 3g protein; 0.9g fibre

Caramelised figs with spiced yogurt

1 cup (280g) low-fat yogurt
¼ cup (35g) roasted pistachios, chopped coarsely
¼ teaspoon ground nutmeg
1 tablespoon caster (superfine) sugar
6 large fresh figs (480g)
1 tablespoon honey

1 Combine yogurt, nuts, nutmeg and sugar in small bowl.
2 Halve figs lengthways. Brush cut-side of figs with honey.
3 Cook figs, cut-side down, uncovered, in heated large non-stick frying pan 5 minutes. Turn figs; cook, uncovered, 5 minutes or until browned.
4 Serve figs with spiced yogurt.

prep + cook time 20 minutes **serves** 4
nutritional count per serving 6g total fat (1.3g saturated fat); 777kJ (186 cal); 26.1g carbohydrate; 6.8g protein; 3.6g fibre

Fig galettes

1 sheet puff pastry
⅓ cup (40g) ground almonds
4 large fresh figs (320g), sliced thinly
30g (1 ounce) butter, melted
2 tablespoons pure maple syrup
2 teaspoons icing (confectioners') sugar

1 Preheat oven to 180°C/350°F. Line oven tray with baking paper.
2 Cut four 12cm (4½-inch) rounds from pastry; sprinkle with ground almonds. Top with figs; brush with combined butter and syrup. Turn edges of pastry up.
3 Bake galettes about 20 minutes or until pastry is puffed and golden. Serve warm, dusted with sifted icing sugar.

prep + cook time 30 minutes **makes** 4
nutritional count per galette 21.4g total fat (5.1g saturated fat); 1446kJ (346 cal); 32.2g carbohydrate; 5.5g protein; 3.4g fibre

Greek coffee

1 cup (250ml) cold water
1 ½ tablespoons ground greek coffee
3 teaspoons caster (superfine) sugar

1 Place the water in 4 demitasse-cup capacity briki or small saucepan. Add coffee and sugar; stir over low heat until sugar dissolves. Slowly bring to the boil; remove from heat when froth almost reaches the top of briki.
2 Divide froth among 4 demitasse cups, then carefully fill the cups with remaining coffee mixture.
3 Serve coffee immediately with a glass of cold water.

prep + cook time 10 minutes **serves** 4
nutritional count per serving 0g total fat (0g saturated fat); 107kJ (26 cal); 6g carbohydrate; 0.6g protein; 0.7g fibre
tip A traditional briki (small pot) is the best pot to use when making Greek coffee because it allows the proper amount of froth to form which in turn adds to the unique taste. Brikis are available from Greek and Middle Eastern delicatessens. A demitasse cup holds about ¼ cup (60ml).

glossary

allspice also called pimento or jamaican pepper; tastes like a combination of nutmeg, cumin, cinnamon and clove. It is available whole or ground from most supemarkets and specialty food stores.

almonds

blanched almonds with brown skins removed.

flaked paper-thin slices.

ground also known as almond meal.

slivered small pieces cut lengthways.

artichoke

globe large flower-bud of a member of the thistle family; it has tough petal-like leaves, and is edible in part when cooked.

hearts tender centre of the globe artichoke; is harvested from the plant after the prickly choke is removed. Cooked hearts can be bought from delis or canned in brine.

baharat also called lebanese seven-spice; an aromatic spice blend, including some or all of the following: mixed spice, black pepper, dried chilli flakes, allspice, paprika, coriander seeds, cinnamon, clove, sumac, nutmeg, cumin seeds and cardamom seeds. It is available from Middle Eastern food stores, some delicatessens and specialist food stores.

baking paper also called parchment paper or baking parchment; a silicone-coated paper primarily used for lining baking pans and oven trays so cakes and biscuits won't stick.

bay leaves aromatic leaves from the bay tree available fresh or dried; adds a strong, slightly peppery flavour.

beans

broad (fava) available dried, fresh, canned and frozen. Peel fresh beans twice – the outer green pod and beige-green inner shell.

lima large, flat kidney-shaped, beige dried and canned beans. Also known as butter beans.

beetroot (beets) firm, round root vegetable.

bicarbonate of soda also called baking soda.

breadcrumbs

fresh bread, usually white, processed into crumbs.

packaged prepared fine-textured, crunchy white breadcrumbs; good for coating foods that are to be fried.

stale crumbs made by grating, blending or processing 1- or 2-day-old bread.

broccolini a cross between broccoli and chinese kale; long asparagus-like stems with a long loose floret, both completely edible. Resembles broccoli but is milder and sweeter in taste.

burghul also called bulghur wheat; hulled steamed wheat kernels that, once dried, are crushed into various sized grains. Used in Middle Eastern dishes such as felafel and tabbouleh. Is not the same as cracked wheat.

butter we use salted butter; 125g is equal to 1 stick (4 ounces).

buttermilk originally the term given to the slightly sour liquid left after butter was churned from cream, today it is commercially made similarly to yogurt. Sold alongside fresh milk products in supermarkets. Despite the implication, of its name it is low in fat.

capers the grey-green buds of a Mediterranean shrub, sold either dried and salted or pickled in a vinegar brine.

capsicum also called bell pepper.

cardamom a spice native to India; can be purchased in pod, seed or ground form. Has a distinctive aromatic, sweetly rich flavour.

cayenne pepper a thin-fleshed, long, extremely hot dried red chilli, usually purchased ground.

cheese

fetta see Greek essentials, page 8

haloumi see Greek essentials, page 8

kasseri a medium hard, mild flavoured sheep-milk cheese (it sometimes has a little goat's milk). It's stringy, rather than crumbly and is great for sandwiches or baking. Can be replaced by provolone.

kefalograviera a hard, salty, sheep or cow-milk cheese. Its flavour is milder than kefalotyri. Can be replaced by pecorino.

kefalotyri a hard, salty cheese made from sheep and/or goat's milk. Its colour varies from white to yellow depending on the mixture of milk used in the process and its age. Great for grating over pasta or salads. Can be replaced by parmesan.

myzithra (fresh) an unsalted, soft Greek whey cheese with a mild flavour, similar to ricotta and farmer's cheese. Other varieties are also available: sour (made with goat's or sheep milk, yeast and salt) and aged (hard and salty).

parmesan also called parmigiano; is a hard, grainy cow's-milk cheese originating in the Parma region of Italy.

ricotta a soft, sweet, moist, white cow-milk cheese with a low fat content and a slightly grainy texture. Its name roughly translates as "cooked again" and refers to ricotta's manufacture from a whey that is itself a by-product of other cheese making.

chicken

drumsticks leg with skin and bone intact.

marylands leg and thigh still connected in a single piece; bones and skin intact.

small chicken also known as spatchcock or poussin; no more than 6 weeks old, weighing a maximum of 500g. Also a cooking term to describe splitting a small chicken open, flattening then grilling.

thigh cutlet thigh with skin and centre bone intact; sometimes found skinned with bone intact.

thigh fillet thigh with skin and centre bone removed.

chickpeas (garbanzo beans) also known as hummus or channa; an irregularly round, sandy-coloured legume. It has a firm texture even after cooking, a floury mouth-feel and robust nutty flavour; available canned or dried (reconstitute for several hours in cold water before use).

chilli use rubber gloves when seeding and chopping fresh chillies as they can burn your skin. We use unseeded chillies because the seeds contain the heat; use fewer chillies rather than seeding the lot.

chocolate, dark eating (semi-sweet) also known as luxury chocolate; made of a high percentage of cocoa liquor and cocoa butter, and little added sugar. Unless stated otherwise, we use dark eating chocolate as it's ideal for use in desserts and cakes.

cinnamon available in pieces (sticks or quills) and ground into powder; one of the world's most common spices, used as a sweet, fragrant flavouring for sweet and savoury dishes.

cloves dried flower buds of a tropical tree; can be used whole or in ground form. They have a strong scent and taste so should be used sparingly.

coconut, desiccated concentrated, dried, unsweetened and finely shredded coconut flesh.

cornichons French for gherkin, a very small variety of cucumber. When pickled, they are the traditional accompaniment to pâté.

cream, pouring we use fresh cream, also called pure cream.

cucumber, lebanese short, slender and thin-skinned cucumber. Has tender, edible skin, tiny, yielding seeds, and sweet, fresh and flavoursome taste.

cumin also called zeera or comino; the dried seed of a plant related to the parsley family. It has a spicy, almost curry-like flavour and is available dried as seeds or ground.

dill used fresh or dried, as seeds or ground, it adds an anise, celery sweetness to foods. Its feathery, frond-like fresh leaves are grassier and more subtle than the dried version or the seeds.

dried currants tiny, almost black raisins so-named after a grape variety that originated in Corinth, Greece. These are not the same as fresh currants, which are the fruit of a plant in the gooseberry family.

eggplant vegetable also called aubergine.

eggs if a recipe calls for raw or barely cooked eggs, exercise caution if there is a salmonella problem in your area, particularly in food eaten by children and pregnant women.

fennel also called finocchio or anise; a crunchy green vegetable slightly resembling celery. Is eaten raw, fried or used as an ingredient in soups and sauces. Also the name given to the dried seeds of the plant which have a stronger licorice flavour.

figs originally from the countries that border the eastern Mediterranean; are best eaten in peak season, at the height of summer. Vary in skin and flesh colour according to type not ripeness. When ripe, figs should be unblemished and bursting with flesh; nectar beads at the base indicate when a fig is at its best.

fillo pastry see Greek essentials, page 9.

flour

plain also known as all-purpose.

self-raising plain or wholemeal flour with baking powder and salt added; make at home in the proportion of 1 cup flour to 2 teaspoons baking powder.

wholemeal also called wholewheat flour; milled with the wheat germ so is higher in fibre and more nutritional than plain flour.

harissa a North African paste made from dried red chillies, garlic, olive oil and caraway seeds; can be used as a rub for meat, an ingredient in sauces and dressings, or eaten as a condiment. It is available from Middle Eastern food shops and some supermarkets.

honey the variety sold in a squeezable container is not suitable for recipes in this book.

kumara (orange sweet potato) the Polynesian name of orange-fleshed sweet potato often confused with yam; good baked, boiled, mashed or fried similarly to other potatoes.

lamb shanks forequarter leg; sometimes sold as drumsticks or frenched shanks if the gristle and narrow end of the bone are discarded and the remaining meat trimmed.

lentils (red, brown, yellow) dried pulses often identified by and named after their colour. Eaten by cultures all over the world, most famously perhaps in the dhals of India, lentils have high food value.

maple-flavoured syrup is made from sugar cane and is also known as golden or pancake syrup. It is not a substitute for pure maple syrup.

maple syrup, pure distilled from the sap of sugar maple trees found only in Canada and about ten states in the USA. Maple-flavoured syrup or pancake syrup is not an adequate substitute for the real thing.

marjoram closely related to and similar in flavour to oregano, but milder and sweeter. A delicious addition to herb mixtures. As with oregano, many chefs prefer dried marjoram to fresh.

mesclun pronounced mess-kluhn; also called mixed greens or spring salad mix. A commercial blend of assorted young lettuce and other green leaves, including baby spinach leaves, mizuna and curly endive.

milk we use full-cream homogenised milk unless stated otherwise.

mizuna Japanese in origin; these frizzy green salad leaves have a delicate mustard flavour.

mushrooms

button small, cultivated white mushrooms with a mild flavour.

portobello are mature, fully opened swiss browns; they are larger and bigger in flavour.

swiss brown also called roman or cremini. Light to dark brown in colour with full-bodied flavour.

nutmeg a strong and pungent spice. Usually purchased ground, the flavour is more intense freshly grated from the whole nut (available from spice shops).

oil

cooking-spray we use a cholesterol-free spray made from canola oil.

olive made from ripened olives. Extra virgin and virgin are the first and second press, respectively, of the olives and are therefore considered the best.

peanut pressed from ground peanuts; the most commonly used oil in Asian cooking because of its high smoke point (capacity to handle high heat without burning).

vegetable from plant rather than animal fats.

okra also called bamia or lady fingers. A green, ridged, oblong pod with a furry skin. Native to Africa, this vegetable is used in Indian, Middle Eastern and South American cooking. Can be eaten on its own; as part of a casserole, curry or gumbo; used to thicken stews or gravies.

olives, kalamata see Greek essentials, page 8

onion

green (scallion) also called, incorrectly, shallot; an immature onion picked before the bulb has formed, has a long, bright-green edible stalk.

red also called spanish, red spanish or bermuda onion; a sweet-flavoured, large, purple-red onion.

spring crisp, narrow green-leafed tops and a round sweet white bulb larger than green onions.

oregano a herb, also called wild marjoram; has a woody stalk and clumps of tiny, dark-green leaves. Has a pungent, peppery flavour.

orzo a small rice-sized pasta. It can be replace by risoni which is slightly smaller.

ouzo an anise-flavoured Greek spirit.

pancetta an Italian unsmoked bacon. Used, sliced or chopped as an ingredient rather than eaten on its own.

paprika ground dried sweet red capsicum (bell pepper); also available sweet, hot, mild and smoked.

pine nuts also known as pignoli; not a nut but a small, cream-coloured kernel from pine cones. They are best roasted before use to bring out the flavour.

pitta bread also called lebanese bread. A wheat-flour pocket bread sold in large, flat pieces that separate into rounds. Also available in small pices called pocket pitta.

polenta also called cornmeal; a flour-like cereal made of dried corn (maize). Also the dish made from it.

potatoes

desiree oval, smooth and pink-skinned, waxy yellow flesh; good boiled, roasted and in salads.

kipfler small, finger-shaped, nutty flavour; good baked and in salads.

lasoda round, red skin with deep eyes, white flesh; good for mashing or roasting.

sebago white skin, oval; good fried, mashed and baked.

prosciutto a kind of unsmoked Italian ham; salted, air-cured and aged, it is usually eaten uncooked.

quail a small, delicate-flavoured farmed game bird related to the pheasant and partridge; it ranges in size from 250g to 300g.

radicchio a red-leafed Italian chicory with a refreshing bitter taste; eaten raw and cooked.

rice

arborio small, round grain rice well-suited to absorb a large amount of liquid; the high level of starch makes it suitable for risottos.

basmati a white, fragrant long-grained rice; the grains fluff up when cooked. It should be washed several times before cooking.

wild not a member of the rice family but the seed of an aquatic grass native to North America. Wild rice has a strong nutty taste and can be expensive, so is best combined with brown and white rices.

rigani see Greek essentials, page 8

risoni small rice-shape pasta; similar to another small pasta, orzo.

roasting/toasting spread nuts and dried coconut evenly on oven tray; roast in moderate oven about 5 minutes. Stir desiccated coconut, pine nuts and sesame seeds over low heat in heavy-based frying pan to toast more evenly.

rocket (arugula) also called rugula and rucola; peppery green leaf eaten raw in salads or used in cooking. Baby rocket leaves are smaller and less peppery.

rosewater extract made from crushed rose petals, called gulab in India; used for its aromatic quality in many sweetmeats and desserts.

saffron the stigma of a member of the crocus family, available ground or in strands; imparts a yellow-orange colour to food once infused. The quality can vary greatly; the best is the world's most expensive spice.

seafood

mussels should only be bought from a reliable fish market: they must be tightly closed when bought, indicating they are alive. Before cooking, scrub shells with a strong brush and remove the beards; do not eat any that do not open after cooking. Varieties include black and green-lip.

octopus are usually tenderised before you buy them; both octopus and squid require either long slow cooking (usually for large molluscs) or quick cooking over high heat (usually for small molluscs) – anything in between will make the octopus tough and rubbery.

prawns (shrimp) can be purchased cooked or uncooked (green), with or without shells.

squid also called calamari; a type of mollusc. Buy squid hoods to make preparation and cooking faster.

white fish fillets means fillets from non-oily fish; includes bream, whiting, ling, flathead, snapper, dhufish and redfish.

semolina coarsely ground flour milled from durum wheat; the flour used in making gnocchi, pasta and couscous.

sesame seeds black and white are the most common of this small oval seed. The seeds are used as an ingredient and as a condiment. Roast in a heavy-based frying pan over low heat.

shallots also called french shallots, golden shallots or eschalots. Small and elongated, with a brown-skin, they grow in tight clusters similar to garlic.

silver beet (swiss chard) also called, incorrectly, spinach; has fleshy stalks and large leaves, both of which can be prepared as for spinach.

sour cream a thick, commercially-cultured sour cream with a minimum fat content of 35 per cent.

spinach also called english spinach and, incorrectly, silver beet.

split peas yellow or green varieties, both with a sweet, strong pea flavour. They are usually pre-soaked but may be cooked without soaking.

sugar

brown a soft, finely granulated sugar retaining molasses for its colour and flavour.

caster also called superfine or finely granulated table sugar.

tahini see Greek essentials, page 9

tomato

bottled pasta sauce a prepared sauce; a blend of tomatoes, herbs and spices.

egg (plum) also called roma, these are smallish, oval-shaped tomatoes much used in Italian cooking or salads.

paste triple-concentrated tomato puree used to flavour soups, stews and sauces.

puree canned pureed tomatoes (not tomato paste).

sun-dried tomato pieces that have been dried with salt; this dehydrates the tomato and concentrates the flavour. We use sun-dried tomatoes packaged in oil, unless otherwise specified.

truss small vine-ripened tomatoes with vine still attached.

vanilla

bean dried, long, thin pod; the minuscule black seeds inside are used to impart a vanilla flavour in baking and desserts.

extract obtained from vanilla beans infused in water; a non-alcoholic version of essence.

vine leaves see Greek essentials, page 9

vinegar

balsamic originally from Modena, Italy, there are now many balsamic vinegars on the market ranging in pungency and quality. Quality can be determined up to a point by price; use the most expensive sparingly.

cider made from fermented apples.

watercress one of the cress family, a large group of peppery greens used raw in salads, dips and sandwiches, or cooked in soups. Highly perishable, so it must be used as soon as possible after purchase.

witlof (belgian endive) related to and confused with chicory. A versatile vegetable, it can be eaten cooked or raw. It is grown in darkness to prevent it becoming green; looks like a tightly furled, cream to very light-green cigar.

yeast (dried and fresh), a raising agent. Granular (7g sachets) and fresh compressed (20g blocks) yeast can usually be substituted for each other.

yogurt we use plain full-cream yogurt.

zucchini also called courgette; small, pale- or dark-green or yellow vegetable belonging to the squash family.

index

A
allspice 386
almonds 386
  almond and walnut pastries (kataifi) 355
  almond biscuits 376
  almond fingers (thaktila) 340
  almond topping, crunchy 79
apricot jam tart 360
artichokes 386
  and asparagus fritters with olive relish 12
  artichoke spinach dip 92
  braised artichokes with crunchy almond topping 79
  broad beans and artichokes 319
  chicken drumsticks with olives and artichokes 204
  fetta and artichoke pizzetta 108
  roast leg of lamb with potatoes and artichokes 268
asparagus
  artichoke and asparagus fritters with olive relish 12
  beetroot, asparagus and fetta salad 176
  haloumi and asparagus bites 72

B
baharat 386
baklava 352
batter 15
  oregano and lemon 24
bay leaves 386
beans 386
  braised borlotti beans with tomato and garlic 308
  braised green beans 320
  braised lamb shanks with white bean puree 284
  broad *see* broad beans
  goat and haricot bean casserole 299
  lamb and lima bean soup 136
  tuna, bean and haloumi salad 168
  white bean puree 284
  white bean salad 155
beef
  beef and fig cigars 119
  meatballs in tomato sauce 120
  zucchini and beef sfougato 68
beetroot 386
  and yogurt dip 96
  beetroot, asparagus and fetta salad 176
  beetroot, pumpkin and spinach salad with fetta polenta 175
  lamb patties with beetroot and tzatziki 292
  roasted beetroot and fetta pizza 107
  salad 59
bicarbonate of soda 386
biscuits, almond 376
biscuits, easter butter (koulourakia) 328
biscuits, honey walnut 348
borlotti beans, braised, with tomato and garlic 308
brandied muscatels 371
brandy yogurt 367
bread, easter (tsoureki) 331
breadcrumbs 386
broad beans 386
  and artichokes 319
  patties with minted yogurt 75
  lemon-pepper lamb with minted broad bean risoni 296
broccolini 386
burghul 386
  burghul, tomato and herb salad 160
butter 386
buttermilk 386

C
cabbage salad 147
cake
  chocolate log 364
  coconut syrup 363
  moist carrot and apple 339
  new year (vasilopita) 324
  pistachio honey 368
  walnut 335
  yogurt 375
calamari 390
  baby, deep-fried 63
  stuffed with fetta and chilli 240
capers 386
capsicum 386
  capsicum, zucchini and orzo salad 144
  char-grilled, salad 227
  eggplant, fetta and capsicum stack with mesclun salad 311
  goat and capsicum stew 275
cardamom 386
carrot and apple cake, moist 339
cayenne pepper 386
cheese 387
  cheese fillo triangles 51
  easter cheese pies (flaounes) 327
  fetta *see* fetta cheese
  haloumi *see* haloumi cheese
  spinach and cheese parcels 52
cheesecake with brandied muscatels 371
cherry spoon sweet 344
chicken 387
  and haloumi skewers with pilaf 208
  and okra stew 196
  barbecued, with minted tomato salad 211
  barbecued lemon thyme chicken 212
  braised, with fennel and ouzo 200
  chicken drumsticks with olives and artichokes 204
  chicken fillo pie 199
  chicken, lemon and rice soup 132
  chicken, tomato and fetta patties with spinach salad 207
  greek chicken and vegetable soup 131
  grilled lemon chicken 216
  lemon and dill chicken 188
  mini chicken souvlakia 104

(*chicken* continued)
oregano chicken with greek salad 215
pilaf 187
roast chickens with dill and walnut pesto 203
roasted garlic, lemon and oregano chicken 184
spicy reddened chicken with pasta 195
chickpeas 387
patties with tahini sauce 39
with banana chillies 304
chilli 387
mint dressing 180
fried chilli prawns with garlic and lemon yogurt 19
chocolate 387
chocolate log cake 364
cinnamon 387
cloves 387
coconut, desiccated 387
coconut syrup cake 363
coffee, greek 384
cornichons 387
cream 388
croquettes, fish 20
cucumber 388
chilled yogurt, cucumber and mint soup 139
tzatziki 31, 292
cumin 388
currants, dried 388
custard tarts, fried 372

D

dill 388
dill and walnut pesto, roast chickens with 203
dips
artichoke spinach 92
beetroot and yogurt 96
eggplant 99
roasted fennel 95
taramasalata 28
tzatziki 31
yellow split pea 27
dolmades 32
dressings 215 *see also* vinaigrette
chilli mint 180
creamy lemon 168
fresh oregano 312
kalamata olive 224

(*dressings* continued)
lemon 159, 160, 176
lemon and basil 163
lemon basil 307
lemony 72
maple orange 164
minted lemon 232
parsley 148
pickled red onion 152
tomato 319
warm walnut 167

E

easter bread (tsoureki) 331
easter butter biscuits (koulourakia) 328
easter cheese pies (flaounes) 327
eggplant 388
and haloumi skewers with roasted tomato sauce 123
deep-fried, with fresh herb sauce 55
dip 99
eggplant, fetta and capsicum stack with mesclun salad 311
eggplant, haloumi and rocket pizza 116
eggplant, tomato and chickpea casserole 303
fritters with garlic yogurt 24
grilled, with marjoram vinaigrette 80
layered vine leaves, eggplant and lamb 288
salad 148
stuffed, with lamb and rice 279
eggs 388

F

fennel 388
and mint salad 252
braised chickens with fennel and ouzo 200
green salad with fennel and herbs 179
oven-roasted fish with braised fennel 228
tomato and fennel sauce 223
fetta cheese 8
and artichoke pizzetta 108

(*fetta cheese* continued)
and spinach stuffed potato balls 16
beetroot, asparagus and fetta salad 176
beetroot, pumpkin and spinach salad with fetta polenta 175
calamari stuffed with fetta and chilli 240
chicken, tomato and fetta patties with spinach salad 207
eggplant, fetta and capsicum stack with mesclun salad 311
grilled fetta and baby truss tomatoes 56
herbed 35
lamb and fetta salad with warm walnut dressing 167
lamb, fetta and spinach fillo parcels 291
lemon fetta toasts 140
prawn, pink grapefruit and fetta salad 180
pumpkin and fetta pide 115
roasted beetroot and fetta pizza 107
seasoned rolled lamb shoulder with fetta and mint 267
spinach and fetta pide 112
spinach, fetta and pine nut salad 159
tomato and fetta toasts 71
figs 388
caramelised, with spiced yogurt 380
galettes 383
quail, fig and orange salad 164
fillo pastry 9
cheese fillo triangles 51
chicken fillo pie 199
lamb, fetta and spinach fillo parcels 291
lamb fillo pie 271
lamb fillo rolls 48
salmon spinach fillo parcels 236
spanakopita 124

(*fillo pastry* continued)
spinach and cheese parcels 52
fish *see* seafood
flaounes (easter cheese pies) 327
flour 388
fritters
artichoke and asparagus, with olive relish 12
eggplant, with garlic yogurt 24
lamb, with spicy yogurt 295
zucchini, with skordalia 15
G
galaktoboureko 356
galettes, fig 383
garlic and lemon potatoes 219
garlic and lemon yogurt 19
garlic confit 287
garlic yogurt 24
goat
and capsicum stew 275
and haricot bean casserole 299
kleftiko 276
greek chicken and vegetable soup 131
greek coffee 384
greek essentials 8–9
greek salad 151
greek-style yogurt 9
green beans, braised 320
green salad with fennel and herbs 179
gyros, fish 239
H
haloumi cheese 8
and asparagus bites 72
barbecued vegetables and haloumi with lemon basil dressing 307
chicken and haloumi skewers with pilaf 208
eggplant and, skewers with roasted tomato sauce 123
eggplant, haloumi and rocket pizza 116
pan-fried 43
prawn and, kebabs 67
roasted vegetable and haloumi salad 163
(*haloumi cheese* continued)
tuna, bean and, salad 168
vegetable and, skewers 100
watermelon and, salad 152
halva 336
harissa 388
herb sauce, fresh 55
herbed fetta cheese 35
honey 388
honey citrus syrup 359
honey walnut biscuits 348
K
kalamata olives 8
dressing, fish steaks with 224
kataifi (almond and walnut pastries) 355
kebabs *see also* skewers
lamb kebabs with yogurt and pitta bread 103
lemon and garlic lamb 263
kleftiko, goat 276
koulourakia (easter butter biscuits) 328
kumara 388
L
lamb 388
and fetta salad with warm walnut dressing 167
and lima bean soup 136
and okra in rich tomato sauce with garlic confit 287
and tomato pide 111
baked, shanks with orzo 255
barbecued, sandwiches 280
braised, meatballs in red wine 300
braised, shanks with white bean puree 284
fried, meatballs 60
lamb cutlets with spinach skordalia 283
lamb, fetta and spinach fillo parcels 291
lamb fillo pie 271
lamb fillo rolls 48
lamb kebabs with yogurt and pitta bread 103
lamb meatballs with egg-lemon sauce 264
lamb patties with beetroot and tzatziki 292
(*lamb* continued)
lamb shanks with lentils 272
layered vine leaves, eggplant and lamb 288
lemon and garlic lamb kebabs 263
lemon-pepper lamb with minted broad bean risoni 296
moussaka 256
pastitsio 259
peppered lamb with watercress, pea and mint salad 171
roast leg of lamb with potatoes and artichokes 268
seasoned rolled lamb shoulder with fetta and mint 267
slow-roasted, with skordalia and potatoes 260
stuffed eggplant with lamb and rice 279
lemon-pepper lamb with minted broad bean risoni 296
lemon thyme chicken, barbecued 212
lemons
and basil dressing 163
and dill chicken 188
and garlic lamb kebabs 263
and garlic yogurt 172
creamy lemon dressing 168
garlic and lemon potatoes 219
grilled lemon chicken 216
basil dressing 307
dressing 159, 160, 176
lemon fetta toasts 140
syrup 355, 356, 363
lemony dressing 72
minted lemon dressing 232
roasted garlic, lemon and oregano chicken 184
lentils
lentil soup 128
lentils, lamb shanks with 272
liver, pan-fried 40
loukoumades 359

M
maple-flavoured syrup 388
maple orange dressing 164
maple syrup, pure 389
marjoram 389
meatballs (lamb) 264
mesclun 389
mezze
  artichoke and asparagus fritters with olive relish 12
  artichoke spinach dip 92
  barbecued baby octopus 84
  barbecued seafood platter 83
  beef and fig cigars 119
  beetroot and yogurt dip 96
  beetroot salad 59
  braised artichokes with crunchy almond topping 79
  broad bean patties with minted yogurt 75
  cheese fillo triangles 51
  chickpea patties with tahini sauce 39
  deep-fried baby calamari 63
  deep-fried eggplant with fresh herb sauce 55
  deep-fried zucchini balls 36
  dolmades 32
  eggplant and haloumi skewers with roasted tomato sauce 123
  eggplant dip 99
  eggplant fritters with garlic yogurt 24
  eggplant, haloumi and rocket pizza 116
  fetta and artichoke pizzetta 108
  fetta and spinach stuffed potato balls 16
  fish croquettes 20
  fried chilli prawns with garlic and lemon yogurt 19
  fried lamb meatballs 60
  grilled eggplant with marjoram vinaigrette 80
  grilled fetta and baby truss tomatoes 56
  haloumi and asparagus bites 72
  herbed fetta cheese 35

(*mezze* continued)
  lamb and tomato pide 111
  lamb fillo rolls 48
  lamb kebabs with yogurt and pitta bread 103
  marinated mushrooms 47
  marinated sardines 64
  meatballs in tomato sauce 120
  mini chicken souvlakia 104
  octopus salad with grilled tomatoes 91
  pan-fried haloumi 43
  pan-fried liver 40
  pickled octopus 88
  pickled vegetables 76
  prawn and haloumi kebabs 67
  pumpkin and fetta pide 115
  roasted beetroot and fetta pizza 107
  roasted fennel dip 95
  saganaki prawns 87
  skordalia 23
  spanakopita 124
  spinach and cheese parcels 52
  spinach and fetta pide 112
  taramasalata 28
  thyme and garlic marinated olives 44
  tomato and fetta toasts 71
  tzatziki 31
  vegetable and haloumi skewers 100
  yellow split pea dip 27
  zucchini and beef sfougato 68
  zucchini fritters with skordalia 15
milk 389
milopita 367
mint
  broad bean patties with minted yogurt 75
  chilled yogurt, cucumber and mint soup 139
  chilli mint dressing 180
  fennel and mint salad 252
  lemon-pepper lamb with minted broad bean risoni 296
  minted lemon dressing 232
  minted tomato salad 211

(*mint* continued)
  minted yogurt 75
  peppered lamb with watercress, pea and mint salad 171
  prawn and zucchini with minted pilaf 232
  salt-baked whole snapper with fennel and mint salad 252
  seasoned rolled lamb shoulder with fetta and mint 267
mizuna 389
moussaka 256
mushrooms 389
  marinated 47
mussel and orzo broth 135
N
new year cake (vasilopita) 324
nutmeg 389
O
octopus
  barbecued baby 84
  octopus salad with grilled tomatoes 91
  pickled 88
  red wine, in 231
oil 389
  rosemary 251
okra 389
  chicken and okra stew 196
  lamb and okra in rich tomato sauce with garlic confit 287
olives
  chicken drumsticks with olives and artichokes 204
  fish steaks with kalamata olive dressing 224
  kalamata 8
  oven-baked fish with tomato and olives 235
  rabbit with olives, parsley and pine nuts 192
  relish 12
  thyme and garlic marinated 44
onion 389
orange spoon sweet 347
oregano 389
  oregano and lemon batter 24

(*oregano* continued)
oregano chicken with greek salad 215
oregano dressing, fresh 312
orzo 389
baked lamb shanks with orzo 255
capsicum, zucchini and orzo salad 144
mussel and orzo broth 135
ouzo 389
braised chickens with fennel and ouzo 200
P
pancetta 389
paprika 389
parsley dressing 148
pastitsio 259
pickled red onion dressing 152
pickled vegetables 76
pickled zucchini salad 156
pide
basic pide dough 111, 112, 115
lamb and tomato 111
pumpkin and fetta 115
spinach and fetta 112
pie
chicken fillo 199
easter cheese (flaounes) 327
lamb fillo 271
pine nuts 389
rabbit with olives, parsley and pine nuts 192
spinach, fetta and pine nut salad 159
squid stuffed with rice, currants and pine nuts 220
pistachio honey cake 368
pitta bread 389–90
pizza
eggplant, haloumi and rocket 116
fetta and artichoke pizzetta 108
roasted beetroot and fetta 107
plums, spiced, with yogurt 379
polenta 390
potatoes 390
fetta and spinach stuffed potato balls 16
fish and potato stew 243
garlic and lemon 219
herbed fish skewers with potato smash and skordalia 247
roast leg of lamb with potatoes and artichokes 268
salt cod and potato pie 248
slow-cooked potatoes with wine and herbs 316
slow-roasted lamb with skordalia and potatoes 260
prawns 390
and haloumi kebabs 67
and zucchini with minted pilaf 232
fried chilli prawns with garlic and lemon yogurt 19
prawn, pink grapefruit and fetta salad 180
saganaki 87
souvlakia with tomato and fennel sauce 223
tomato and oregano 244
prosciutto 390
pumpkin
beetroot, pumpkin and spinach salad with fetta polenta 175
pumpkin and fetta pide 115
Q
quail 390
quail, fig and orange salad 164
R
rabbit
olives, parsley and pine nuts, with 192
rabbit stifado 191
radicchio 390
red wine, braised lamb meatballs in 300
red wine vinaigrette 179
relish, olive 12
rice 390
chicken and haloumi skewers with pilaf 208
chicken, lemon and rice soup 132
(*rice* continued)
chicken pilaf 187
prawn and zucchini with minted pilaf 232
pudding with cinnamon and vanilla bean 351
squid stuffed with rice, currants and pine nuts 220
stuffed eggplant with lamb and rice 279
wild rice salad with lemon and garlic yogurt 172
rigani 8
risoni 390
lemon-pepper lamb with minted broad bean risoni 296
risoni salad 203
rocket 290
rosemary oil 251
rosewater 390
S
saffron 390
saganaki prawns 87
salad
beetroot 59
beetroot, asparagus and fetta 176
beetroot, pumpkin and spinach salad with fetta polenta 175
burghul, tomato and herb 160
cabbage 147
capsicum, zucchini and orzo 144
char-grilled capsicum 227
eggplant 148
fennel and mint 252
greek 151
green, with fennel and herbs 179
lamb and fetta, with warm walnut dressing 167
minted tomato 211
octopus, with grilled tomatoes 91
peppered lamb with watercress, pea and mint 171
pickled zucchini 156
prawn, pink grapefruit and fetta 180

(*salad* continued)
quail, fig and orange 164
risoni 203
roasted vegetable and haloumi 163
spinach, fetta and pine nut 159
tuna, bean and haloumi 168
watermelon and haloumi 152
white bean 155
wild rice salad with lemon and garlic yogurt 172
salmon spinach fillo parcels 236
salt-baked whole snapper with fennel and mint salad 252
salt cod and potato pie 248
sandwiches, barbecued lamb 280
sardines, barbecued vine-leaf-wrapped 219
sardines, marinated 64
sauce
fresh herb 55
lemon yogurt 208
roasted tomato 123
tahini 39
tomato and fennel 223
white 256
seafood 390
barbecued, platter 83
barbecued vine-leaf-wrapped sardines 219
calamari stuffed with fetta and chilli 240
crisp-skinned fish with roast garlic skordalia 251
deep-fried baby calamari 63
fish and potato stew 243
fish croquettes 20
fish gyros 239
fish steaks with kalamata olive dressing 224
herbed fish skewers with potato smash and skordalia 247
marinated sardines 64
mussel and orzo broth 135
octopus in red wine 231
oven-baked fish with tomato and olives 235
(*seafood* continued)
oven-roasted fish with braised fennel 228
prawns *see* prawns
salmon spinach fillo parcels 236
salt-baked whole snapper with fennel and mint salad 252
salt cod and potato pie 248
squid stuffed with rice, currants and pine nuts 220
taramasalata 28
tuna, bean and haloumi salad 168
tuna souvlakia with char-grilled capsicum salad 227
semolina 391
sesame seeds 391
shallots 391
silver beet 391
skewers *see also* kebabs
chicken and haloumi skewers with pilaf 208
eggplant and haloumi skewers with roasted tomato sauce 123
herbed fish skewers with potato smash and skordalia 247
vegetable and haloumi 100
skordalia 15, 23, 247, 260
roast garlic 251
spinach 283
soups
chicken, lemon and rice 132
chilled yogurt, cucumber and mint 139
cream of spinach soup with lemon fetta toasts 140
greek chicken and vegetable 131
lamb and lima bean 136
lentil 128
mussel and orzo broth 135
sour cream 391
souvlakia
mini chicken 104
prawn, with tomato and fennel sauce 223
tuna, with char-grilled capsicum salad 227
spanakopita 124
spiced plums with yogurt 379
spiced syrup 348
spicy reddened chicken with pasta 195
spinach 391
and cheese parcels 52
and fetta pide 112
artichoke spinach dip 92
beetroot, pumpkin and spinach salad with fetta polenta 175
chicken, tomato and fetta patties with spinach salad 207
cream of spinach soup with lemon fetta toasts 140
fetta and spinach stuffed potato balls 16
lamb, fetta and spinach fillo parcels 291
salmon spinach fillo parcels 236
skordalia 283
spinach, fetta and pine nut salad 159
split peas 391
yellow split pea dip 27
squid stuffed with rice, currants and pine nuts 220
stew
chicken and okra 196
fish and potato 243
goat and capsicum 275
stifado, rabbit 191
sugar 391
summer vegetable terrine 315
sweets
almond and walnut pastries (kataifi) 355
almond biscuits 376
apricot jam tart 360
baklava 352
caramelised figs with spiced yogurt 380
cheesecake with brandied muscatels 371
cherry spoon sweet 344
chocolate log cake 364
coconut syrup cake 363
fig galettes 383

(*sweets* continued)
fried custard tarts 372
galaktoboureko 356
greek coffee 384
honey walnut biscuits 348
loukoumades 359
milopita 367
orange spoon sweet 347
pistachio honey cake 368
rice pudding with cinnamon and vanilla bean 351
spiced plums with yogurt 379
yogurt cake 375
syrup 335, 352
honey citrus 359
lemon 355, 356, 363
spiced 348

T

tahini 9
sauce 39
taramasalata 28
tart, apricot jam 360
tarts, fried custard 372
thaktila (almond fingers) 340
thiples (deep-fried sweet pastries) 332
thyme and garlic marinated olives 44
tomatoes 391
braised borlotti beans with tomato and garlic 308
braised green beans 320
burghul, tomato and herb salad 160
chicken, tomato and fetta patties with spinach salad 207
dressing 319
eggplant and haloumi skewers with roasted tomato sauce 123
eggplant, tomato and chickpea casserole 303
grilled fetta and baby truss tomatoes 56
lamb and okra in rich tomato sauce with garlic confit 287
lamb and tomato pide 111
minted tomato salad 211
octopus salad with grilled tomatoes 91

(*salad* continued)
oven-baked fish with tomato and olives 235
tomato and fennel sauce 223
tomato and fetta toasts 71
tomato and oregano prawns 244
tsoureki (easter bread) 331
tuna, bean and haloumi salad 168
tuna souvlakia with char-grilled capsicum salad 227
tzatziki 31, 292

V

vanilla 391
vasilopita (new year cake) 324
vegetables *see also* by individual name
and haloumi skewers 100
barbecued, and haloumi with lemon basil dressing 307
braised borlotti beans with tomato and garlic 308
broad beans and artichokes 319
char-grilled, with fresh oregano dressing 312
chickpeas with banana chillies 304
eggplant, fetta and capsicum stack with mesclun salad 311
eggplant, tomato and chickpea casserole 303
pickled vegetables 76
roasted vegetable and haloumi salad 163
slow-cooked potatoes with wine and herbs 316
summer, terrine 315
vinaigrette *see also* dressings
red wine 179
walnut 175
white wine 171
vine leaves 9
dolmades 32
layered vine leaves, eggplant and lamb 288
vinegar 391

W

walnuts
cake 335
kataifi (almond and walnut pastries) 355
vinaigrette 175
warm walnut dressing 167
watercress 391
watermelon and haloumi salad 152
white bean puree 284
white bean salad 155
white sauce 256
white wine vinaigrette 171
wild rice salad with lemon and garlic yogurt 172
witlof 391

Y

yeast 391
yellow split pea dip 27
yogurt 391
beetroot and yogurt dip 96
brandy 367
cake 375
caramelised figs with spiced yogurt 380
chilled yogurt, cucumber and mint soup 139
garlic 19, 24
greek-style 9
lamb fritters with spicy yogurt 295
lemon and garlic 172
lemon yogurt sauce 208
minted 75
spiced plums with 379
tzatziki 31

Z

zucchini 391
and beef sfougato 68
capsicum, zucchini and orzo salad 144
deep-fried, balls 36
fritters with skordalia 15
pickled zucchini salad 156
prawn and, with minted pilaf 232

conversion chart

MEASURES

One Australian metric measuring cup holds approximately 250ml, one Australian metric tablespoon holds 20ml, one Australian metric teaspoon holds 5ml.

The difference between one country's measuring cups and another's is within a two- or three-teaspoon variance, and will not affect your cooking results. North America, New Zealand and the United Kingdom use a 15ml tablespoon.

All cup and spoon measurements are level. The most accurate way of measuring dry ingredients is to weigh them. When measuring liquids, use a clear glass or plastic jug with the metric markings.

We use large eggs with an average weight of 60g.

LIQUID MEASURES

METRIC	IMPERIAL
30ml	1 fluid oz
60ml	2 fluid oz
100ml	3 fluid oz
125ml	4 fluid oz
150ml	5 fluid oz (¼ pint/1 gill)
190ml	6 fluid oz
250ml	8 fluid oz
300ml	10 fluid oz (½ pint)
500ml	16 fluid oz
600ml	20 fluid oz (1 pint)
1000ml (1 litre)	1¾ pints

LENGTH MEASURES

METRIC	IMPERIAL
3mm	⅛in
6mm	¼in
1cm	½in
2cm	¾in
2.5cm	1in
5cm	2in
6cm	2½in
8cm	3in
10cm	4in
13cm	5in
15cm	6in
18cm	7in
20cm	8in
23cm	9in
25cm	10in
28cm	11in
30cm	12in (1ft)

DRY MEASURES

METRIC	IMPERIAL
15g	½oz
30g	1oz
60g	2oz
90g	3oz
125g	4oz (¼lb)
155g	5oz
185g	6oz
220g	7oz
250g	8oz (½lb)
280g	9oz
315g	10oz
345g	11oz
375g	12oz (¾lb)
410g	13oz
440g	14oz
470g	15oz
500g	16oz (1lb)
750g	24oz (1½lb)
1kg	32oz (2lb)

OVEN TEMPERATURES

The oven temperatures in this book are for conventional ovens;
if you have a fan-forced oven, decrease the temperature by 10-20 degrees.

	°C (CELSIUS)	°F (FAHRENHEIT)
Very slow	120	250
Slow	150	300
Moderately slow	160	325
Moderate	180	350
Moderately hot	200	400
Hot	220	425
Very hot	240	475

First published in 2011 by ACP Magazines Ltd,
a division of PBL Media Pty Limited
54 Park St, Sydney
GPO Box 4088, Sydney, NSW 2001.
phone (02) 9282 8618; fax (02) 9267 9438
acpbooks@acpmagazines.com.au; www.acpbooks.com.au

ACP BOOKS
General Manager - Christine Whiston
Associate publisher - Seymour Cohen
Editor-in-Chief - Susan Tomnay
Creative Director & Designer - Hieu Chi Nguyen
Food Director - Pamela Clark

Published and Distributed in the United Kingdom by Octopus Publishing Group
Endeavour House
189 Shaftesbury Avenue
London WC2H 8JY
United Kingdom
phone (+44)(0)207 632 5400; fax (+44)(0)207 632 5405
info@octopus-publishing.co.uk;
www.octopusbooks.co.uk

Printed by Toppan Printing Co., China

International foreign language rights, Brian Cearnes, ACP Books bcearnes@acpmagazines.com.au

A catalogue record for this book is available from the British Library.
ISBN 978-1-74245-107-7